CANDLE MAGIC

CANDLE MAGIC

Working with Wax, Wick & Flame

BY

LADY PASSION

HIGH PRIESTESS, COVEN OLDENWILDE

STERLING ETHOS
New York

STERLING ETHOS
New York

An Imprint of Sterling Publishing Co., Inc.
1166 Avenue of the Americas
New York, NY 10036

ISBN 978-454-2708-2

Distributed in Canada by Sterling Publishing Co., Inc.
c/o Canadian Manda Group, 664 Annette Street
Toronto, Ontario, Canada M6S 2C8
Distributed in the United Kingdom by GMC Distribution Services
Castle Place, 166 High Street, Lewes, East Sussex, England BN7 1XU
Distributed in Australia by NewSouth Books
45 Beach Street, Coogee, NSW 2034, Australia

For information about custom editions, special sales, and premium and corporate purchases,
please contact Sterling Special Sales at 800-805-5489 or specialsales@sterlingpublishing.com.

Manufactured in the United States

2 4 6 8 10 9 7 5 3 1

sterlingpublishing.com

✤ Cover Design by Jo Obarowski ✤
♣ Interior design by Gavin Motnyk ♣

Interior image credits
Depositphotos.com: © lavalova: 11; iStock: © hiorgos: 69, © ilbusca: 82,
© ivan-96: 5, © jpa1999: 98, © Tatanata: 143; Smithsonian Institution:
123; Courtesy Wikimedia Commons: 39

DEDICATION

To flame Gods

and bold folk who yearn to work

effective ash, fire, heat, light, liquid metal, smoke, solar, and wax magic.

CONTENTS

INTRODUCTION

"The mind is not a vessel to be filled, but a fire to be kindled."

—Plutarch

A blazing hearth that imparts content . . . a bubbling cauldron that brews a Witches' flying ointment . . . incense tendrils of curling smoke that reveals future events . . . an entrancing balefire that teases you to juggle its coals . . . a liquor-lit centerpiece of dancing blue flames—these and similar experiences explain our fascination with the Element Fire's mysterious allure and mystical virtues.

Fire is mutable—its fractal flames bedazzle us with their rainbow palette and speak to us with vigorous gusto or in a humming sizzle as they tire of their antics and fizzle out with languor. The recognizable symbols and images that fire produces are never static but instead change, dissolve, and re-form in unpredictable ways that reveal its life force of enthusiasm, impulsivity, and greediness for more wood, wax, or wick.

Many these days see fire only in its most glaring expression as the dynamic ther-monuclear hub of our particular solar system among the many in our arm of the Milky Way.

Pagans, though, have celebrated our Sun as a life-sustaining deity for millennia, particularly at His zenith during the summer solstice when His proximity to Earth is closest, and at His nadir during the winter solstice, when He is farthest away.[1] Early Christians spurned ancient Pagan astronomy and thus, Theodosius in 386 C.E decreed every Sunday holy.[2]

Fire is unique—no two fires burn in identical fashion. Flames are spooky; they look, act, and, Witches maintain, *are alive*, animated with individual and collective spirit.

Fire creates, sustains, and kills—little can reproduce, germinate, or grow with-out proper heat to enable its complex functions. We have figurative "fire in our belly": body temperature that fluctuates throughout our lifetime. Fire's power is evident when we're feverish or outraged—nurse a grudge, attack, or rail against injustice—and it feels

---

1 During the Litha and Yule Sabbats, respectively.
2 *Codex* fragment II.8.18. Many Witches consider it an affront to be forced to mark time by the Christian saint-based "Gregorian" calendar versus its precursor, the Pagan lunar-based "Julian" calendar. We revere so many ancient God/desses that we find it ludicrous to reckon time on the basis of a single male, desert-dwelling deity's unknown birth date ages hence. Instead of appending our dates with B.C. (Before Christ) or A.D. (Anno Domini; Year of God, associated with Jesus's crucifixion), we use the inclusive B.C.E. (Before the Common Era) or C.E. (Comman Era, modern times).

transcendent when we copulate or warm to high praise. Death results when we can't regulate our thermochemical processes or escape exposure to temperature extremes.

Compelled or perhaps destined to rebel, fire razes vast swaths (wildfires), boils sea floors (black chimneys), and causes planet-wide weather catastrophe (ice ages that follow the eruption of a super-volcano or fiery meteor strike). Witches respect fire's boon and bane nature and continue to magically utilize the long-demonized Element to wreak magical wonders.

Each spark that we nurture requires deft care to prevent it from loosening its insatiable appetite to consume. Little wonder that Wisefolk have worked fire magic for eons, for it takes wits to "feed the baby," a phrase that aptly describes the patient, tinder-to-log method of starting a fire from scratch. Even as newborns don't eat steak, Witches coax fire into being by using airy wood shavings and gradually increasing the density and size of combustibles until wee flames burgeon into an awe-inspiring blaze.

In contrast, the concept of "building" a fire reveals the approach-avoidance attitude with which many people have come to approach the primal Element. Many of us have been raised watching the media malign fire—news crews bashing its destructive capability, lamenting its unpredictable, indiscriminate, voraciousness nature, its difficulty to "contain," and the almost smug devastation it leaves behind. Wildfire is most typically described as the manifestation of the wrath of Mother Nature versus an act of God or human fault (arson, exploding gas lines, people building homes in a drought plain, etc.).

The truth is that fire has enabled the evolution of all living creatures. Plants developed spores to take advantage of it, trees grew woody bark to minimize its effect, and animals developed fleet feet, thick hides, and keen smoke smell to detect its imminent danger. The earliest human footprints discovered to date are thought to have been formed by someone dancing around a fire atop wet cave clay.[3]

Initial civilizations burned sacred fires in temples to promote continuity, honor the Sun, attract strength, and inspire hope during bleak times. For centuries Pagans drove their livestock between fires or torches to imbue the beasts with solar health, and lit fires on high places to mark Sabbat festivities or warn nearby tribes of plague or invasion.

Just as modern folk use mutable plastic in infinite ways, the ancients used fire to liquefy metals for weapons; steam-shape wood for warships and wheels; to fumigate sickrooms; and to purify brackish water.

---

3 In Chauvet Cave, France.

Many people were paid to lovingly make and tend torches of rushes and reeds, glean hedgerows for tinder, render animal fat into candles, and slice peat like an art form. Indeed, until as little as 150 years ago, humanity's first question about almost anything encountered was "Can it burn?"

Everything that could be burned *was*, to foster a sense of safety, to promote spirituality, and to maximize productivity. In fact, Pagans were so closely associated with firelight that upstart, self-styled rival monotheist cults felt compelled to claim it was a sinister vice and began to literally demonize fire by transforming the Goddess Hel's frigid Underworld Afterlife realm into Satan's eternal lake of fire.[4]

Some not only took their Elemental benefactor for granted, but perverted it to suit nefarious plans. Punitive laws were passed forbidding anyone but the nobility and their minions from collecting firewood on their landholdings. Conquerors and soldiers burned down enemy villages and later burned alive those they loathed or feared, such as the philosopher Giordano Bruno, heretics such as the Cathars and Albigensians, Witches by order of the Inquisition, and later still, gypsies by Nazis.

At the height of the Burning Times, Witches adapted to pain of death by casting pentacles of melted wax to signify the four Quarter directions of their ritual circles, hopeful that if their practices were discovered, the pentacles could be quickly pitched Frisbee-style into a fire and all evidence of their devilment duly destroyed.

During the Industrial Revolution, chimney soot cast a polluted pall over major cities, further tainting fire's traditional virtues in inhabitants' hearts and minds.

Even as fire melted steel for railroad tracks, trains, cars, and skyscrapers, horrid workplace conditions made many *fear* fire increasingly—to view it with suspicion and to denigrate it as being primitive, inefficient, and inconvenient.

Millennia of legalized terrorism when overlords and oppressors could burn anyone to death so scarred humanity's collective unconscious that governments today routinely threaten perceived enemy counties with "bombing them back to the Stone Age," using fiery weapons of mass destruction such as napalm, drone air strikes, and laser arrays in space, imperiling all life with extinction from stockpiles of aging, non-secured nuclear warheads and leaking barrels of toxic incendiary liquids.

A recent example is the 1996 movie featuring the 14 wild land firefighters who succumbed on Storm King Mountain, Colorado, on July 6th, 1994, the film's actress portraying a reporter labeling fire "the eternal enemy."

---

4 A traditional Witch insult to intolerant, persecutory monotheists is "May they burn in the Hell of the Christians."

Few formerly positive words and phrases associated with fire, such as "beacon" and "keep the home fires burning," remain in common use today. But perhaps Mother Earth is firing back in ire because wildfires and global warming rage, increasingly reducing ill-conceived grass plain and hillside mega-mansions to rubble.

Witches are as much inclined to rebel, to go against the grain of corrupt society, as the Element fire itself. We never embrace its vainglory or potential for monetary gain, nor gain power at others' expense, and thus we remain fiercely entranced by the sacred Element's pure power. Indeed, Pagans are so enraptured by fire that we value having an embarrassment of riches in the form of possessing an abundance of candles and incense to light for every conceivable magical need or mundane desire.

We adore fire's sensuality—the way it imparts sophistication, encourages introspection, prompts ardent declarations of love, and promotes convivial contentment. We delight in the amorphous shadows it casts that connect us with the ancients. We thrill to the way it provokes us to dance until we reach ecstasy or achieve catharsis.

Witches perpetuate many fine fire magic traditions, such as melting wax into poppets of people to heal them or bind them from doing harm. We use it to brew potent potions, flying ointments, and herbal medicines. We leap fire to conjure health, wealth, peace, strength, luck, joy, and fertility; use it to transmute metal into magical tools and talismans; burn parchment spells to send our will spiraling aloft to ethereal deities; and offer lit offerings of candles and incense to cultivate and appease the Gods when we feel grateful, regretful, grieved, contrite, and in need of Their largesse.

Books abound that encourage readers to achieve their dreams by doing things in ways taught by specific systems from Catholicism to Candomblé, and there's nothing wrong with this. Unfortunately, most tomes patronize readers by regurgitating pithy principles previously printed a thousand times, leaving readers cold who yearn for legitimate depth of material that would allow them to harness true firepower.

Beyond their insulting simplicity, this ilk is oft irreverently lax ("Feel free to use a plastic lighter."[5]), impedingly restrictive ("Buy a huge copper brazier."[6]), or downright dangerous ("Blow out the candle."[7]).

Some encourage spellcrafters to work fire magic only on a Sunday in honor of the Sun God or in contrast, to burn anything anytime the mood strikes them regardless of whether it's astrologically auspicious or undercuts their ritual spell intent.

---

5 As explained in *The Goodly Spellbook: Olde Spells for Modern Problems*, plastic negates magic.
6 You don't have to bust your budget to acquire rare ingredients to work powerful magic.
7 No Witches worth their salt would risk offending the spirit of the Element by using their profane breath to extinguish pure fire: instead, we use a ceremonial metal candle-snuffer.

Candle Magic: Working with Wax Wick & Flame reveals magical answers to burning questions about fire arts—burn magic that you won't find anywhere else. Mesmerizing true tales of fire rites from my ongoing decades as the High Priestess of the traditional Gardnerian Coven Oldenwilde show readers how to courageously command combustibles.

This illustrated bombshell reveals the piquant Pagan domain of fiery decor, foods, and fashions; fire Sabbat and celebration times, ideas, and menus; candle, cauldron, and lamp spells; fire Elementals, entities, Spirits, and deities; insider tips on cold-fire options; smoke, soot, and ash magic; and much more.

Relish the power of confidently leaping a cauldron fire or dancing with lit poi. Learn how to cast shadows even in darkness and how to foretell the future by focusing on flickering flame. Feel calm while swaddled in the relaxing warmth of a bonfire—the smoke of hardwood wafting skyward, entrancing you in a dreamlike state or transporting you to other realms or timelines. Enjoy finding items you already have or can acquire inexpensively that will inspire romance or electrify friends' and loved ones' flagging energy. Above all, thrill in the pleasure of becoming a *Witch aglow*— a Wise One who can use simple candles and fire to help yourself and others thrive!

—Lady Passion, High Priestess,
Coven Oldenwilde

COLD-FIRE MAGIC:
WHEN YOU CAN'T BURN FLAME

"If I read a book and it makes my whole body so cold no fire can ever warm me,
I know that is poetry."

—Emily Dickinson

Working fire magic can feel very challenging if you live with bigoted family members who disapprove of Paganism or are the tenant of a landlord who forbids burning candles. Flame may be prohibited because you're young, live in a dorm, or live with someone who uses flammable oxygen to breathe. You may be a blind Solitary Witch and find that the beauty of flame is superfluous or poses a safety risk when you are practicing magic alone.

SCENTS, SPICES, AND CUISINE

To subliminally manipulate consumers, grocery stores, real estate agencies, brick-and-mortar stores, restaurants, and craven entrepreneurs engage in "ambient scent technology": They routinely perfume themselves, the air in their business places, and their produce, property, products, and packaging with subtle or blatant notes of all-spice, cardamom, cinnamon, clove, nutmeg, and similar aromas that evoke in the brain a subconscious childhood sensory feeling of trust, desire, or pleasure associated with eating freshly baked cookies or apple pie, etc.

This is called "sensory marketing," and corporations are saturating home paper goods essentials from paper towels and toilet paper, to magazine and book pages, and hygiene products with the stuff; even heating pads are impregnated with cinnamon.[8]

Real estate agents, salespeople, and front-line workers often wear hearth-scented

---

8 *The Science of Sensory Marketing* (Harvard Business Review, March 2015).

perfume or essential oil featuring smoky notes and undertones, spray property for sale on the open market or the products they're pitching, and impregnate paper and plastic packaging with scents that neurologists, biologists, and chemists contend exert involuntary effects on the psyche that can provoke impulse buying.

In order to elicit, direct, and ensure long-term consumption of their product, businesses employ string lights, chandeliers, wall sconces, black lights, strobe lights, colored lampshades, lava lamps, lanterns, tiki torches, battery-operated tea lights, stained glass, painted lightbulbs, and more.

Scent is a powerful human sense, and a case can be made that it is a more subjective one in many ways than sight, hearing, or taste experiences that can be more readily vetted by witnesses or documented and reconsidered later. Some can't abide the sight of blood, whereas health-care workers may be nonplussed by it; others can't stand a crying baby, whereas parents may tune it out or instinctively respond to it; and most people describe the smell of feces or decomposition as repugnant.

As with all magic, it matters what you absorb in your mind and what you choose to inhale in your surroundings: Few people want to live near facilities that process coal, burn tires, discharge toxic chemicals, or spew reek that goes wherever the wind blows.

Yet many who consider themselves mainstream have become apathetic, effectively rendered "nose-blind" by the constant and increasing inundation of the artificial scents that they're bombarded with—a milieu of everything from building paint and detergents to new car smell. Oppositely, it's a Pagan point of pride to recognize and reject this type of craven manipulation or restriction of our options. We prefer to surround ourselves with natural scents to evoke a mood or to magically correspond with and support our spell intentions.

Still, some don't like what we find natural: the ancient sacred smell of burning incense. Some equate it with smoking cannabis; others claim that it is done solely to disguise the burning of a rock of crack cocaine and the like, or insist that lighting a stick or cone of compressed resin telegraphs a radical ideology such as Rastafarianism.

Regardless of such people's assumptions or rationale, if you find yourself banned from burning incense or are temporarily unable to afford it but want to incorporate scent in some way to achieve magic success, you can substitute any or all of the following:

* INFUSE YOURSELF: Immerse yourself in a bath of stimulating herbs or spices such as lemongrass inside a knot-closed, loosely woven linen fabric scrap,[9] a cotton tea-steeping pouch, or even a metal tea ball.

* HUMIDIFY YOUR ENVIRONMENT: Simmer fiery herbs or spices in a pot of water atop a turned-on stove burner.

* FUMIGATE YOUR HOME: Diffuse fiery-scented essential oil throughout the air by pouring some into any small dish or shot glass and putting it on a windowsill or in the well of a lamp reservoir that sits atop a lit lightbulb.

* I often put essential oil in a small Japanese sake vase and then insert plain wooden skewers readily available for a dollar per pack of a hundred in grocery stores. The oil defies gravity and wicks upward through the wood's vertical fibers, subtly infusing a room for months.

* ANOINT YOUR VALUABLES AND PROTECT YOUR VULNERABILITIES: Animate or add magical *oomph* to your decor, entrances and exits,[10] regalia, ritual garb or tools with the magical power of the Element fire by thrice anointing them with a fire essence,[11] using your right forefinger.[12]

* TO NEGATE FIERY INFLUENCE—say, the wrath of a handsy boss who can withhold your paycheck if you rebuff his sexual harrassment—use your *left* forefinger to thrice anoint yourself using the ole prostitute secret for repelling advances: lavender oil.

As you can see, there's much you can do to infuse your life with the magical scent influence of fire. Bless or blast, cure or curse as the need arises or you feel inclined, by using ingredients that smell, taste, or evoke a sense of fire without having to burn anything.

There's no limit to exploring fire's possible permutations, but you'll fare best in the long run if you master magical correspondences of the Element as explained and illustrated in *The Goodly Spellbook, as well as* the ancient Pagan Cardinal Virtues as explained in *Rituals & Sabbats*. In the latter example, the Cardinal Virtue of justice

---

9 Such as the kind used to strain liquids while cooking.
10 Like mouths, orifices and entry vectors for infection such as wounds, home entryways, and open doors and cabinets are innately vulnerable to invasion and are best kept closed and sealed. Open cabinets invite rumors against you. Anointing doors, windows, and chimney openings protects families from invasion or unwanted and unwelcome visitors, relatives, and unsolicited salesfolk.
11 Distillate, dust, or oil of an herb or spice.
12 Ruled by the largest planet in our solar system, Jupiter, the forefinger packs a whopping magical punch. Mundanely, it is used to stress a point during debate, or to accuse another during an argument.

equates with the Element fire, the South quarter, and with the Witch Power to Will. Impulsive Will is selfish and, hence, unjust: instead, you can exercise fiery volition to Will justice for the good of everyone by working spells and being involved in spiritual activism.

Even though you're only working with representations of fire, you'll *still* be trying to accomplish what you would by burning—namely, to do any or all of the following and similar things:

* To cultivate spontaneity.

* To conjure the courage to take audacious action.

* To prevail during a conflict with someone.

* To increase your stamina.

* To become sexually adventurous.

* To be more loving toward others.

* To strengthen your willpower.

Blend your own signature sultry scent to wear in order to stay alert at a mind-numbing job or to feel sexy in preparation for a hot date. Many occult supply stores and online shops offer peppery essential oils with names like "Hot Tamale" or "Come-Hither," but Witches often prefer to make our own, such as by adding powdered cinnamon or cinnamon sticks to a liquid base of clear mineral oil. You can use any hot spice that you're not allergic to in order to make an essential oil this way, depending on your scent preference and magical intention. Simply use the spice(s) sparingly to prevent an unanticipated allergic reaction or a burning sensation.

Similar to this, I once used cinnamon oil to anoint participants into circle, and they all ended up sporting a red spiral temporary tattoo on their forehead! During the Cakes & Wine ceremony after the rite, we laughed picturing how it might look like blood to a cop if they were pulled over on their way home: "Honestly ossifer, I'm not a Manson family member, it's just cinnamon oil."

Increase the magical effect that your sizzling scent will exert by wearing copper or brass jewelry and orange, red, rust, or maroon clothing. Garner triple power by doing this on Tuesdays or from midnight Saturday through Sunday.

Thwart winter doldrums by cooking and sharing a meal featuring herbs, spices, and meals that induce a bead or two of sweat.

Hot edible spices include the following:

Acidic reeds	Coriander	Nettles
Cayenne	Dill	Nutmeg
Chilies	Garlic	Peppercorns
Chili powder	Ginger	Peppers
Chipotle	Lemongrass	Smoky paprika

Savory foodstuffs and piquant cuisines include the following:

Brazilian dishes	Japanese food	Shallots
Cajun foods	Kimchi	Szechwan food
Chili	Korean food	Tangy worts and weeds
Gumbo	Leeks	Thai food
Horseradish	Mexican food	Vietnamese food
Hot sauce	Onion	Wasabi paste

We gypsies, Witches, and Pagans are renowned for our sultry scents, our exotic herb wiles with the wame,[13] and our ways of making stone soup banquets out of next to nothing.

We love it all: picking, drying, distilling, bottling, and surrounding ourselves with alluring scents; seeding, plucking, preserving, and infusing our scoper[14] with spices; and pickling, slicing, cooking, and ingesting nutritious comfort food.

AROMATIC ARRANGEMENT
Delight your sight and energize your ambience by making a magical centerpiece featuring fire textures, colors, and components.

---

13 A Witch word meaning stomach, as in "he was saxed in the wame" or axed in the gut.
14 A Witch word meaning supper.

INGREDIENTS: Natural items that magically correspond with red-hot fire, such as *pungent sticks, kindling strips, spiked tree cones, spice-scented potpourri, red Chinese lantern pods, dried tri-color peppercorns, molted cardinal feathers, curls of copper wire and a bowl*
DIRECTIONS: *Find, gather, or repurpose items in a bowl and use it as a centerpiece.*
OPTION: *Spritz ingredients with a spicy essential oil.*

APHRODITE APHRODISIAC

This is a simple-to-make herbal tincture that ignites passion and promotes bonding and camaraderie.

INGREDIENTS: *Moonshine or vodka; dried damiana herb; clear jar with rubber-seal top; tincture bottle*
DIRECTIONS

Half fill a clean clear Mason jar or a similar glass container with dried damiana plant matter. Deluge with liquor base of choice to brim such as vodka. Lightly rubber seal the jar top, shake thoroughly, and label and date the contents. Store in a dry, dark place for 21 or more days.

When the virtues of the plant have been duly extracted by the liquid base, strain the plant matter and store the liquid in a tincture bottle, cap tightly, and label and date the contents.

Although damiana wine is readily available, it is not nearly as potent as damiana in extracted tincture form. Ingest as drops under your tongue. Determine your dose by the way it makes you feel—typically open, relaxed, and convivial.

CIDER COCKTAIL

This is a tasty folk remedy immune booster that you can make as a "simple"[15] or a "compound."[16]

INGREDIENTS: A liquid base of apple cider vinegar; you may add brandy, cognac, gin, moonshine, Schnapps, or anything similar; dried hot-sour herbs or spices of choice; clear jar with rubber-seal top; label; and tincture bottle or dispensing vessel.

DIRECTIONS:

Half fill any clean, clear glass vessel with whole dried herb(s) or fill it $1/4$ to $1/3$ with powdered spice(s) of choice. Deluge with equal parts apple cider vinegar and liquor of choice to the brim. Rubber-seal cap, shake thoroughly, and label and date contents. Loosen cap and keep the brew in a dry, dark place for a minimum of 21 days. Afterward, strain clean of plant matter, bottle the liquid, cap tightly, and label and date the contents.

Many folk fail to appreciate herbal meds because their faith flakes on the shoals of their doubt about its efficacy, or they may balk at the raw taste. But if you are rightly Witch-hardy, forfend illness by ingesting this undiluted brew sublingually (in drops under your tongue) or swigging it by the dram shot. Self-titrate the dose by drinking drops by the cupful each day until symptoms abate. Cease if they persist or if you experience an unpleasant side effect. Herbs don't work as fast as pharmaceuticals; they work gently over time.

Alternatives: Include powdered peppermint or dried tarragon.

DANGLING DIVINATION

Foretell future events or see how faraway friends or relatives fare.

DIRECTIONS:

Tie together fresh fiery herb sprigs using hemp, twine, or other sting, and suspend each bunch twig-end up, blossoms down from your ceiling or a high place indoors. If they dry evenly without sporting black spots, all will be well for you and all's well with the one you love or wonder about; if the leaves mold or shed, your spell results are portentous and may necessitate spellwork to minimize negative events in your or their future.

If only one sprig molds, appeal to the Gods for aid. If two or more sprigs wither, cast a spell of protection on their behalf.

---

15 A preparation featuring a liquid base and only one herb or spice.
16 A preparation that includes either several bases mixed or one base and several herbs or spices that work synergistically (ingredients whose body actions support one another rather than antagonize or cancel out each others' effects).

LAVA LOVE FEAST

This easy-to-make menu sparks explosive passion.

Menu

COCKTAIL: Cinnamon scotch

APPETIZER: Breadsticks with honey–hot sauce dip

ENTRÉE: Paprika ham with chipotle carrots and chili powdered red bell peppers

DESSERT: Tart cherries

DIGESTIF: Peppered chocolate coffee

INGREDIENTS: Scotch; two cinnamon sticks; breadsticks; hot sauce; honey; ham; smoky paprika; carrots; chipotle; chili powder; red bell peppers; tart cherries (fresh or canned-glazed); coffee; chocolate syrup; cracked black pepper; clear dishes; tall tea-stirring spoons; and coffee mugs

DIRECTIONS:

Brew coffee. Add a cinnamon swizzle stick to room-temperature scotch and serve in a clear glass. Vertically drop store-bought breadsticks into a clear lager glass. Add drops of hot sauce into honey and pour into two clear shot glasses in which to dip breadsticks.

Cover washed ham with smoky paprika. Cut carrots into coins and vertically slice red bell peppers. Place ham in roaster. Spice carrot coins with chipotle, and red pepper slices with chili powder. Sprinkle carrots and peppers around around the ham. Cover the roaster and bake per package directions.

Serve tart cherries at room temperature in two clear pudding dessert glasses or two champagne flutes. Use long tea-stirring spoons to eat the cherries. Pour coffee into (preferably) red mugs, drizzle in chocolate, and add cracked black pepper atop to suit.

The cinnamon swizzle sticks, breadsticks, long tea-stirring spoons, and sliced red bell peppers symbolize the male phallus, and the tart cherries symbolize the female labia. Revel in the romance!

PROVOCATIVE POPPET

Attract a mate by making a wax doll that represents you.

INGREDIENTS: A hot plate or stove; two pots, one larger than the other; one solid pink or red taper candle; tongs; a piece of paper; a piece of wax paper; a sexy essential oil; and a soft or pink cloth (a bath rag will suffice)

DIRECTIONS:

Fill the larger pot with water so that the smaller pot won't tip over or spill when you put it inside the larger pot. Turn on your heat source. When the water boils, melt the candle in the smaller pot. When the wax is melted, turn off the heat source and cool the pots.

Use the tongs to remove the wick from the melted candle wax and place it on the paper. The paper represents the kinds of paper that couples share, from a marriage certificate to money and bills, and the wick stands for the tie that binds lovers. Bury both later with a wish for a love that lasts.

When the molten wax is cool to the touch, massage it into a palm-size figure that resembles your physique (svelte, husky, or rotund, etc.). As you do this, speak sweetly to it, for it's a magical simulacrum, or version of yourself. Call it by your name and say how you want your mate to view and treat you, how you want to act in a relationship, and what you expect and won't tolerate in a lover. When you are done, let the *ding-ding darling* (a Witch word meaning poppet doll) dry completely atop the wax paper.

Afterward, remove the wax paper and bathe the poppet from head to toe in the sexy essential oil. Wrap it gingerly in a soft pink cloth and house it in the South direction in the home where you bide.

After sunset on any Friday, the weekday sacred to the Norse love Goddess Freya, magically work your poppet by verbally reiterating your desires. When the Gods grant your heart's desire, give Them an offering in thanks, but never tell your love how you attracted them. Don't break up your poppet or your health may suffer: instead, keep it hidden in the North/Earth direction so no one else can magically work you.

FIRELESS LIGHTING ALTERNATIVES

When I was barely 13, I was relegated to using my closet as a ritual space because my fundamentalist adoptive parents despised Witchcraft.

At first, I cast about for a way to evade their raptor-like scrutiny enough to lay down some real magic, but I soon devised myriad enabling ways that worked for me, but kept them utterly unaware of my daily magic. In time, I even took a sort of fiendish delight in my ability to pull the wool over their eyes.

For example, my Protestant folks abhorred candles because they were bigoted against Catholics, and so they forbade me to burn wax (indeed, I never saw a single candle in the house the entire 15 years I lived there).

Undeterred, I bought four sheer scarves in the Elemental colors of red, green, yellow, and blue from the local five-and-dime store. Then, whenever I wanted to cast a spell, I simply selected the appropriately colored scarf and wrapped it around my closet's light fixture so that I was bathed in light that corresponded to my magical intention. My method was silent, odorless, and effective; best of all, it prevented detection and the horrid *afterclap*[17] that would have resulted.

You need not be suppressed in your choice of using magical fire options to decide that you need or want to use alternative lighting. There are many reasons that might incline you to seek an alternative to open flame.

Reasons include the following:

* Your town or venue forbids open flame because it doesn't want the liability risk. (I've successfully protested this, by the way.)

* You want to permeate a rite with a specific color, such as purple pink that is difficult for a typical fire to achieve.

* You plan to elaborately decorate tabletop altars and don't want to risk ruining your tablecloths with candle drips or accidentally set your arrangements ablaze.

* The outdoor area in which you planned to host a huge gathering or ritual is suddenly designated a "do not burn" zone because of extended drought and windy conditions.

* You don't want to buy a ton of candles only to have them break during transport to the ritual.

* Your circling site is sloped, and there's no flatland on which to secure candles or torches upright safely.

In these and similar situations, substitute inexpensive battery-operated LED[18] tea lights. These abound online, and you can order them so that their flickering simulated flame tips will emit just the type of color you want to use to evoke a particular feeling in your rites or spellworkings.

The base of many LED tea lights sport seasonal colors and graphics such as orange with black Halloween Witches flying atop broomsticks. Or you can do what

---

17 A Witch word meaning negative consequences.
18 Light-emitting diode.

I do and buy less expensive white ones and use a permanent ink marker to decorate their housing with mystical signs and symbols in colors that suit your magical purpose.

I often use this cold-fire alternative in tandem with conventional open flame to light the nighttime public and Coven rites that I conduct, and I always keep several on each Quarter altar in my ritual room as well. The varying layers of diverse lighting delight the eyes more than anything I could achieve if I relied on a uniform kind.

LED tea lights are a perfect alternative for prison inmates who are forbidden to burn candles (wrongly, I contend) or for hospitalized folk to use in lieu of burning healing candles in a highly flammable oxygenated environment.

Battery-operated tea lights can burn for days to weeks, and their underside teensy coin-like batteries are often replaceable; some are even available in a dock for recharging. Each comes with a pre-installed battery, and multi-packs often include a few extra batteries to allow for replacement if a couple of tea lights lose their charge from being stored for too long before being ordered and shipped.

Consecrate "not plastic" lights by anointing the base of each one with an essential oil that suits your spell purpose.

In the same vein as LED tea lights is the glow-stick family of fluorescent lighting. Also called snap-sticks and popularized by ravers, this alternative lighting option is also plastic and comes in all manner of lengths, colors, and styles, including jewelry (bracelets, necklaces, rings, crowns, etc.), and in the form of musical instruments such as tambourines. Suppliers can even print your event's name and date on hundreds of them to make it a prized souvenir of your magical event.

To activate the chemical inside, glow-stick technology requires only a snap between two hands—no need to contend with batteries. However, just as for LED tea lights, I typically spare myself this extra expense by decorating blank snap-sticks using a permanent ink marker. I've given out thousands to participants in my rituals over the decades so that every attendee has his or her own personal lighting in addition to what I provide in ambience.

For more options, such as how to make a hanging glow-stick lantern using only four tarot cards, a hole punch, and embroidery floss, reference *The Goodly Spellbook: Olde Spells for Modern Problems*.

For indoor workings there are even more alternative lighting options, such as plugging in drippy electric Yule lights or a Star Shower®—type laser that casts a cosmic pattern in different colors throughout the room.

Perhaps my personal favorite alternative spell lighting options are screw-in black light bulbs. Black light is widely available in large spherical bulbs or horizontal glass cylinders of varying lengths. Their lunar light flatters Witch faces and glints off our lovely garb, regalia, and decor much better than does the typical ghastly orange or green Halloween light.

Other indoor options are to decorate ceilings with plastic glow-in-the-dark stars, or to use shimmery, reflective fabrics.

STAINED GLASS BULB SPELL

Easily make your own magical light to enhance indoor rites and spells or highlight ritual room Quarters!

INGREDIENTS: Clear glass light bulb; erasable marker; arts-and-crafts squeeze bottle "liquid lead" (in black, silver, or copper to suit); squeeze bottle "transparent glass stain"; vise grip or something similar to hold the bulb upright while working and drying; drip catcher (newspaper or something similar).

DIRECTIONS:

Delicately tighten bulb base in vise. Apply desired design atop glass with erasable marker until satisfied. Squeeze liquid leading atop design lines. Air-dry. Fill in between leading lines your desired transparent glass stain. Air-dry. Screw in bulb and enjoy your Witchy handiwork.

COLD-FIRE SPELLS

Conjure fire through silent prayer or gesture or through chanting, employing the opposite Element—water—and cool-touch flame.

Throughout this book I give ancient grimoire spells from Persia, Egypt, and Greece, often written in Old Coptic. In contrast with modern folks' convention of listing the ingredients before a recipe, the providers of these magical formulas oft appended preparation instructions as if they were hastily scribbled to enable the success of an inexperienced Initiate or spellcaster.

Ignore the spells' occasionally inapt pronouns, breathy grammar, and erratically capitalized and lowercase *voces magicae*.[19] Their vowel-consonant strings represent deity names, nature tones, and music of the spheres (the sounds that spinning

---

19 Magical voices, typically God/dess sacred names or epithets chanted, bigraved on a candle, or written on parchment to compel divine aid. *The Goodly Spellbook* is replete with spells featuring them—what Witches call "Barbarous Words of Power".

planets emanate). Intone them as practice reveals a rhythm to you, or as you would pronounce Greek:[20]

"CH" as "ach" as in Scotish "loch"

"E" as a long English "a"

"O" like English "oh"

"OU" like English "oo"

"PH" as "p" or "f"

"TH" as "t" or "th"

"Y" like a German umlaut "u"

If you are awestruck during the spellwork, do as the ancients did and pepper your words with "hissings," "poppings," or other discordant sounds.[21]

Enjoy the reward of true power that the ancients provide!

SUN SALUTE

The following ancient spell from the *Papri Graecae Magicae (PGM)* III. 1–59[22] has many magical applications.

You can use it to adore the Sun at its rise, zenith, or demise[23] to incline the orb during dreary weather; to forfend rain at Pagan festivals adoors; to help heal yourself of injury or gloom; and to imbue yourself and others with vitality and stamina.

I included the traditional Selene salute to the Moon in *The Goodly Spellbook.* I suggest that in the following spell you combine intoning the two Barbarous Words below with outwardly raising your fist—a clenched hand being an olde Witch gesture to conjure the Power to Will. This is identical to the Black Panther gesture of resistance.

The address to the sun/requires nothing except:

"IAEOBAPHRENEMOUN" and the formula "IARBATHA."

---

20 For a more in-depth tutorial, reference the Greek pronunciation illustration in the chapter "Secret Writing—Letters, Glyphs, and Runes," *The Goodly Spellbook.*

21 Source, second-century C.E. musician and mystic Nicomachus.

22 Magical material contemporary with the Chaldean Oracles, *Papryi Graecae Magicae* is the name given to a cache of ancient Persian-Greco-Roman spells on papyrus and bigraved on iron "curse" tablets collected by Jean d'Anastaisi in Egypt in the early nineteenth century but not fully published until 1925. Although translator Hans Dieter Betz conjectured that d'Anastaisi may have discovered them in a tomb or temple library, and that the largest collection of papyri may have been in the private collection of a magician in Thebes, their precise provenance remains a mystery. *PGM* brackets are a scribe's unless specified as a translator's or my own.

23 At sunrise, noon, and sunset.

APHRODITE SAUCER DIVINATION

Summon a sultry Goddess to reveal happenings from afar. The following spell from *PGM* IV.3209–54 uses Aphrodite's antithesis to visibly manifest Her fiery aspect.

Practice purity for seven days in advance. You can prepare the required magical myrrh ink by pulverizing the resin and thinning it with water.[24]

Having kept oneself Pure for 7 days,[25] take a White Saucer,[26] fill It with Water and Olive Oil, having previously written on Its Base with Myrrh Ink: "E'IOCH CHIPHA ELAMPSE'RZE'LA E E' I O Y O"; and beneath the Base, on the outside[27]: "TACHIE'L CNTHONIE DRAXO." Wax over with White Wax. On the outside of the Rim at the Top (write once and then thrice intone): "IERMI PHILO' ERIKO'MA DERKO' MALO'K GAULE' APHRIE'L I ask." Let It rest on the Floor and looking intently at It, say "I call upon You, the Mother and Mistress of Nymphs, ILAOCH OBRIE' LOUCH TLOR; Come in, Holy Light, and give Answer, showing Your Lovely Shape!"

Then look intently at the Bowl. When you see Her, welcome Her and say, "Hail, Very Glorious Goddess, ILARA OUCH. And if You give me a Response, extend Your Hand."

And when She extends It, expect Answers to your Inquiry. But if She does not listen, say, "I call upon the ILAOUCH who has begotten Himeros, the Lovely Horai and You Graces; I also call upon the Zeus-sprung Physis[28] of All Things, two-formed, indivisible, straight, foam-beautiful Aphrodite. Reveal to me Your Lovely Light and Your Lovely Face, O Mistress ILAOUCH. I conjure You, Giver of Fire, by ELGINAL, and by the Great Names OBRIE'TYCH KERDYNOUCHILE'PSIN NIOU NAUNIN IOUTHOU THRIGX TATIOUTH GERTIATH GERGERIS GERGERIE" THEITHI. I also ask You by the All Wonderful Names, OISIA EI EI AO' E'Y AAO' IO'IAIAIO' SO'THOU BERBROI AKTEROBORE GERIE' IE'OYA; bring me Light and Your Lovely Face and the True Saucer Divination, You shining with Fire, bearing Fire all around, stirring the Land from afar, IO' IO' PHTHAIE' THOUTHOI PHAEPHI. Do it!"

PREPARATION: Having kept yourself Pure, as you learned, take a Bronze Drinking

---

24 *PGM* I.232-47 specifies myrrh ink as "Myrrh Troglitis, 4 drams; 3 Karian Figs, 7 pits of Nikolaus Dates, 7 dried Pinecones, 7 piths of the single-stemmed Wormwood, 7 wings of the Hermaic Ibis, Spring Water." Substitute similar ingredients for the figs and dates and bird or peacock feathers for ibis wings.

25 Rather than a body/matter mortification act favored by monotheists, ancient Pagans viewed purity as an overt sign of reverence when one was approaching the Gods. To them, purity meant having abstained from meat and uncooked food; abstain only from sex and masturbation if the spell specifies.

26 White divination vessels are hard to scry, and the Preparation section below conflicts with this by specifying a bronze cup. I recommend using copper because it is the metal that magically corresponds with Aphrodite/Venus.

27 This implies atop a flat surface on which you put the bowl, in conflict with the Preparation section below, which specifies atop the knees. You could write this on parchment and place it under the bowl on your knees (folded legs while sitting on a floor).

28 Nature of.

Cup, and write with Myrrh Ink the previously inscribed Stele charm or amulet which calls upon Aphrodite, and use the untouched Olive Oil and clean River Water. Put the Drinking Cup on your Knees and speak over it the Stele mentioned above, and the Goddess will appear to you and will reveal concerning what Things you wish.

BLUE COLD-FIRE SPELL

The following fire begins red-orange hot but then turns cool blue as its combustible liquid evaporates: My Covenmates and I often gracefully weave our hands in and out of its flames.

To enable us to sit and scry atop cushions or leap the fire as we wish, we oft put the ingredients in a smallish iron cauldron inside a larger potbelly model. Feel free to substitute an elevated censer, and if you don't like the acrid scent, fumigate and ventilate (burn incense and open a window).

DIRECTIONS:

Half fill a small to medium-size iron cauldron with Epsom® salts and level the granules. Drench with 70 to 90 percent isopropyl "rubbing" alcohol 1/2 to 1 inch (1.27cm to 2.54cm) above the top of the salt line. Briefly let the salts absorb the liquid; then light and relish.

The remains are not goodly to compost, so dispose of them in the trash. Rinse the cauldron with water, and, if you are using a metal censer, pat it dry. Re-season the cauldron by slathering vegetable shortening on the affected areas and heating it on low in an oven until the coating melts clear. Let it air-cool. Replace the use-ready Witch tool in your circling space.

ALTERNATIVE: Appeal for deity aid by imbibing moonshine: if it is pure, 'twill burn blue if set alight.

HELIOS MEMORY AMULET

One way that Witches magically attract what we desire is by repelling what's known to impede it. The following spell from *PGM* III.410-23 operates by this Pagan principle of antipathy[29] by propitiating the Moon Goddess Selene so that she does not blunt memory, and thus enables the Sun God Helios to ensure it.

To conjure a memory you lack, fast on a Sunday. After sunset, use a gold-colored stylus to etch an Egyptian eye of Horus on silvery metal and then work the spell.

Take a silver Tablet and engrave it with the uzait horn, or "Sacred Eye of

---

29 Fully explained in the section "How the Art Magical Works," *The Goodly Spellbook*.

Horns"[30] after the God, e. g., Helios, when the Sun sets. Take cow's milk and pour it or, perhaps heat it. Put it into a clean vessel and place the tablet under it. Add barley meal, mix, and form bread: twelve rolls in the shape of female figures.[31] Say the formula three times, eat the rolls on an empty stomach, and you will know The Power.

The formula: "BORKA BORKA PHRIX PHRIX RIX O' . . . ACHACH AMIXAG OUCH THIP LAI LAI LAMLAI LAI LAM MAIL AAAAAAAA IIIY E'l AI O'O'O'O'O'O'O' MOUMOU O'YIO' NAK NAK NAX LAINLIMM LAILAM AEDA . . . LAILAM AE'O O'AE' O'AE' E'OA' AO'E' E'O'A O'E'A, enter, Master, into my Mind, and grant me Memory, MMM E'E'E' MTHPH!"

Consecrate the lamella with the Element Air[32] by passing it through incense smoke. Forfend general forgetfulness by wearing the ingot as a pendant; absorb information with ease by suspending it in your study space, library, or computer office; retain what you learn or experience by sleeping atop the amulet, which is kept under your pillow; and promote instant recall by fondling it in your pocket.

Follow through by performing the second part of the spell:

Do this monthly, facing the Moon, on the First Day of the month: Prostrate yourself before the Goddess, e. g., Selene, the moon, and wear the Tablet as an Amulet.[33]

NOTUS KNOT SPELL

Notos (Greek) is one of the four Venti, or wind Gods, associated with the four directions. Spelled Notus in Gardnerian Witchcraft, He is the hot South wind that blows northward and personifies fire by the force of His rains. Hesiod mentions Him first among His peers as being "a great blessing to man."[34]

If drought stretches from late summer into early autumn, magically break it by appealing to Notus to send rain that will enable the Mabon Sabbat fruit, vegetable, and grain harvest.

DIRECTIONS:

On a Sunday at sunrise (optimally during a waxing or full moon), sit facing the South direction and powder frankincense resin by using a mortar and pestle or putting it inside a double layer of paper bags and banging it to bits with a rubber mallet.

---

30 Sic, Uzat/wadjet/eye of Horus, not a horn.
31 Such as a diamond-shaped "Venus of Willendorf."
32 Magically associated with mind/memory.
33 An amulet is a natural item that is innately magical without human intervention. In this spell the silver is bigraved, resulting in a talisman.
34 *Theogony* 869.

Take a piece of string or clothesline in hand and tie a knot for each hardship that you can think of that continued drought would pose, such as wildfires, shriveled crops, higher food prices, and famine. Then untie each knot while visualizing needful saturation, fleshy fruits and vegetables, plump loaves of bread, colorful autumn leaves, and the like. Rock back and forth; really *feel* your power to summon a God to keep weather balanced and humane.

Roll the string in the frankincense—get pieces in the crevices. See each tiny crystal as a drop of warm rain nourishing where it is needed and will land. See the line as a connection from Notus in the sky to the rain He will send to you, the conjurer on humanity's behalf: a straight line from A to B if you will. As you crystallize the strand, intone the following ancient paean spell:

> "*To Notos (the South Wind),*
> *Fumigation from Frankincense.*
> *Wide-coursing gales,*
> *whose lightly leaping feet*
> *with rapid wings*
> *the air's wet bosom beat,*
> *approach, benevolent,*
> *swift-whirling powers,*
> *with humid clouds*
> *the principles of showers;*
> *for showery clouds*
> *are portioned to your care,*
> *to send on earth*
> *from all-surrounding air.*
> *Hear, blessed power,*
> *these holy rites attend,*
> *and fruitful rains on earth*
> *all-parent send.*"[35]

Tie the resin rain-bringer string onto the branch of a tree in the South direction, letting most of it dangle in the wind.

---

35 Orphic Hymn 82 to Notus.

SOLAR MAGIC SQUARE TALISMAN

When you would have the power of the Sun bless your endeavors, find the illustration of the star's magic square in *The Goodly Spellbook*. Face the South and burn an orange candle and frankincense. Draw the grid number square using lemon juice or red ink on nice parchment or paper stock.

Iron the double roundel between two sheets of wax paper. Cut off excess paper around the square. Fold it like a compact. Keep it close by or use it as a focus during meditation or solar rites.

ANTI-WILDFIRE, BURN AND FEVER CURES, AND SOLAR SPELLS

The following are burn-curing, fever-breaking, fire-stopping, and healing solar spells from a 19th-century German grimoire, the 1828 English translation frontispiece of which bears the flowery title *Johanm Georg Hohman's Pow-Wows; Or, Long Lost Friend: A Collection Of Mysterious And Invaluable Arts And Remedies, For Man As Well As Animals, With Many Proofs of their value and efficacy in healing diseases, ect, [sic]* the greater part of which was never published until they appeared in print for the first time in the U.S. in the year 1820. I give them numbered and as appeared, spelling and grammar errors "as is," explanatory brackets and footnotes mine.

A VERY GOOD REMEDY FOR THE WILDFIRE

Thrice intone:

> *"Wild-fire and the dragon,*
> *flew over a wagon*[36]
> *The wild-fire abated,*
> *and the dragon skated."*

If fire should break out unexpectedly, then try to get a whole shirt in which your servant-maid had her terms or a sheet on which a child was born,[37] and throw it into the fire, wrapped up in a bundle, and without saying anything. This will certainly stop it.

---

36 Wagons of hay and combustibles that caught fire were believed overflown and set alight by a fire-dragon. This is a classic ill averted by saying its *opposite* spell—the spellcaster acknowledges the likelihood of fire, but declares that the majority of flammables in the wagon were spared, the dragon flew off elsewhere.

37 In other words, bloody sheets from a menstruating virgin, or those stripped from a childbirth bed. Magically, this embodies the "water puts the fire out" Pagan principle, and shows the deeply personal nature of the fire danger.

HOW TO BANISH THE FEVER

Write the following words upon a paper parchment and wrap it up in knot-grass, (breiten Megrieb,[38]) and then tie it upon the body of the person who has the fever:

Potmat sineat,

Potmat sineat,

Potmat sineat.[39]

A REMEDY FOR EPILEPSY, PROVIDED THE SUBJECT HAS NEVER FALLEN INTO FIRE OR WATER

Write reversedly or backward upon a piece of paper parchment:

IT IS ALL OVER!

This is to be written but once upon the paper; then put it in a scarlet-red cloth, and then wrap it in a piece of unbleached linen,[40] and hang it around the neck of the sufferer on the first Friday of the new moon. The thread with which it is tied must also be unbleached.[41]

A REMEDY FOR BURNS

Say:

"Burn, I blow on thee!"

It the burn must be blown on three times in the same breath, like the fire by the sun.[42]

HELIOTROPE (SUNFLOWER): A MEANS TO PREVENT CALUMNIATION[43] [SIC]

The virtues of this plant are miraculous. If it be collected in the sign of the lion Leo, in the month of August, and wrapped up in a laurel leaf together with the tooth of a wolf.[44]

---

38 Buckwheat or dock. If you lack this, substitute twitch-grass, five-finger grass, or knot any tall grass.

39 This talisman spell features Witches' traditional use of Barbarous Words of Power and numerological triplicity—two keys to magical mastery.

40 Or substitute an unbleached cotton tea-steeping pouch.

41 In Friend spells means make the sign of the four Quarters of the circle using your thumbs, either after an invocation, or on the person, or on the magical object.

42 . . . "like the sun" means forcefully, similar to quick Lamaze childbirth breaths.

43 To accuse falsely, trick, maliciously slander.

44 Humanely harvested wolf teeth are available at occult supply stores, or substitute a similar natural sharp tooth or obsidian arrowhead, etc.

Whoever carries this about him or her, will never be addressed harshly by anyone, but all will speak to him or her kindly and peaceably.

And if anything has been stolen from you put this under your head during the night, and you will surely see the whole figure of the thief. This has been found true.

TO EXTINGUISH FIRE WITHOUT WATER

Write the following words on each side of a plate, and throw it into the fire, and it will be extinguished forthwith:

SATOR

AREPO

TENET

OPERA

ROTAS[45]

PEACHES

Like oranges and grapefruit, peaches resemble the Sun. The flowers of the peach-tree, prepared like salad, open the bowels, and is of use in the dropsy.[46]

Six or seven peeled kernels of the peach-stone,[47] eaten daily, will ease the gravel;[48] they are also said to prevent drunkenness, when eaten before meals.

Whoever loses his or her hair should pound up peach kernels, mix them with vinegar, and put them on the bald place.[49]

The water distilled from peach flowers opens the bowels of infants and destroys their worms, e.g., intestinal parasites.

---

45 Interestingly, also used in To Be Given To Cattle Against Witchcraft (e.g., to prevent them being bewitched).
46 Relieves constipation and reduces edema, such as swollen eyes or legs, or congestive heart failure.
47 In other words, remove the outer fruit from the peach pits.
48 In antiquity variously called gallstones, venereal disease, and epilepsy.
49 Sympathetic magic-wise, solar peaches are fuzzy outside, and have red, veinous-like fibers that resist pit removal from the fruit inside. Vinegar is astringent and hence, the recipe cleanses the scalp and magically improves blood flow to hair follicles.

FIRE FLIRTING: THE BLESSING AND BLASTING POWERS OF LIGHT, HEAT, AND FIRE

"I am going to notice the lights of the earth, the sun and the moon and the stars, the lights of our candles as we march, the lights with which spring teases us, the light that is already present."

—Anne Lamott, author and progressive political activist

F ire magic is as infinite as human experience and ingenuity. Fall under its spell and raise your magic to a higher level; no genius or diploma is required to master its primal secrets. The Element's range promises traditional survival skills and beautiful ways to expand your talents, express your spirituality, and revel in your magical might.

Fire has many magical correspondences: associations such as love and hate, passion and sabotage, blood and roses.[50] Pagans respect the fact that this Element's aspects can bless or blast, heal and kill. A force extreme, sunlight can provide vitamin D or cause melanoma, grow grapes fat or desiccate the vine, cure chilblains or cause heatstroke, ease coughs or suffocate, flame-prep fields or wither entire crops, and spark romance or lead to pregnancy.[51]

Witches work light, heat, smoke, and flame magic in ways that run from raw to intricate. For examples, prisms that cast rainbows, faceted crystals hung on window-panes to catch and spray sunlight, and light streaming through curtains of colorful sliced agate delight all who enter my Covenstead.

Bathing patients in pale yellow light stimulates healing far more rapidly than keeping them in shadow or surrounded by brilliant white electric light. Steeping tea, simmering wine, oils, herbs, and piping-hot feast foods evoke memories of home and inspire feelings of trust and belonging. Comforting wood smoke and sultry incense

---

50 Reference many more in the section "Four Elements and Four Quarters," *The Goodly Spellbook*.
51 Reference the Attraction spell "For a Woman to Conceive" in *The Goodly Spellbook*.

set a mystical mood. Lit liquor, lanterns, and a dazzling array of flickering candles elevate expectation of Witch Mysteries that imminent circle rites will reveal.

Since Witches know that blowing out fire offends the Element, we extinguish it by pinching it out with a forefinger and thumb, cupping our hands and clapping it out, or smothering it out with a candlesnuffer.

Pagans also often flirt with fire: We twiddle our fingers through the bottom, blue part of the flame, merrily freaking folks out with our seeming imperviousness to burning. For example, when *Diuvei and I were asked by traditional British fans of The Goodly Spellbook to teach at Pendle Witch Camp in England in 2006, we were thrilled and amazed by the wild fire magic some troupes performed after the main summer solstice ritual. They danced with fire, spun it, ate it, and tossed it in ways that most Americans would never dare try. The entertainment was a transfixing, empowering rite in itself.

Mastering fire's complexity begins by learning its manifestations on a personal level. Watch the sun shine through tree leaves while you rest atop the ground on your back: they resemble stained glass. Walk barefoot in high summer and feel heat's intensity on pavement and diverse surfaces. Listen to the crackle, pop, and hiss of a campfire. Notice how each candle flame has a personality, is tall or short, and flickers in different directions. Look for the shapes that tendrils of incense smoke form.

Anyone can connect with nature this way, and parents in particular can dispel both the fire fear common in children and the fire bravado common to teens by involving their offspring in fun fire activities.

Fire safety drills' focus on avoidance can breed fear in kids, and their repetition desensitizes teens to its danger. In contrast, sharing magical fire experiences can imbue youngsters with confidence and take the shock value out of teenage pyromania.

Beyond whether kids should be allowed to work fire magic (of course they should), many fire questions abound.

Some worry that burning candles and magical fires depletes ozone (less so than burning fossil fuel oil and gasoline). Others wonder if one gender has a natural affinity for working fire magic better than that of the other (no, I've seen an angry girl conjure lightning out of thin air and a fire-scrying boy foretell the future as well as any adult, but certainly those born in the fiery astrological signs of Ares, Leo, and Sagittarius have a special innate talent for it).

Still others wonder if "natural" candles composed solely of soy, palm oil, or beeswax are magically superior to typical candles from stores (no, as any candle can be consecrated for spell use; however, it is most efficacious to acquire candles that are saturated with color *throughout* versus buying candles with a white core and that only sport a thin outer layer of color.

Yet others worry that their spell may be ruined if they move a lit candle even if only to prevent it from setting their circle ablaze (possibly; changing a lit candle's position alters its burn and drip pattern, and so your spell and omen results may change accordingly—best to set candles properly from the start to avoid the need to move them).

Don't fret if you lack a candle in the color the spell requires: substitute white or red. White is always acceptable, inexpensive, and readily available. Red is the default alternative color that Gardnerian Witches use in lieu of having Quarter candles in the color that corresponds to the direction: East, white or yellow; South, red, pink, or orange; West, blue, turquoise; North, green, black, or brown. We equate red with the blood of birth, the fiery Witch Power to Will, and more.

What does it mean when a lit candle crackles or hisses, burns in bizarre shapes, or snuffs itself out? The meaning of this is based on common sense and is easy to figure out.

First, consider each candle's appearance: Could its wick benefit from being trimmed, pulled aright, or sheltered from a draft? Would it prefer being lit with a match instead of a lighter? Closely espy it and let it tell you what it prefers or needs.

Crackles connote drought or derision from others. Hisses portend imminent rain or jealous treachery by others. Embers that spit off the wick mean that emotion and energy are high—magic's afoot, but be alert for danger or secret agendas.

The shapes that flames assume and that candle wax drips make have meaning deserving of interpretation and heeding. They are one of the many means that the God/desses use to communicate wisdom, warning, and foresight to us, and they manifest in symbols that we can recognize.

For instance, a candle that snuffs itself out soon after being lit may simply have a crooked wick that previously melted into the top of the wax. In that case, pull it up vertically and then relight it. Check your wicks before every rite or spell to ensure that all are upright.

The spirit of a flame may be resistive to being burned or, by being burned, may show that the Gods either don't support your spell or don't want the candle to be lit at that moment. In that case, take the hint as you would a flower that fights your plucking of it. Try lighting a different candle.

You can unleash light, heat, and fire's innate powers to bless and cure life forms by applying each or a combination of them as needed, but always judiciously, wisely, deftly—say, by exposing someone sick to sunlight/vitamin D at high noon on a Sunday, or putting insulating cover over plants threatened with frost on a cold winter's Saturday night.

Yet as with all Elemental balance, light, heat, and fire also can be used to blast or repel an enemy, to curse, or even to kill. Too mighty a solar flare cast-off and the planet would be desiccated, become desert waste, and we could roast from lethal radiation. For eons now diverse armies have adopted a "scorched earth" policy of burning fields as they fled or conquered as an easy means of forcing their foes to lose by attrition caused by starvation.

Tribes and corporations have burned off vast rain forest reserves of incalculable long-term value for short-term monetary gain. Bumper stickers proliferate that sport the plaintive question "Daddy, what did a tree look like?"

Obviously, burning on a grand scale threatens us all, but there may come a time when you want to work with these forces to magically oppose an injustice. For instance, you may decide to use bright illumination in a ritual to literally "shed light" on or expose an inequality or wrong done to you or your loved ones.

Witches often work such spells to oppose the offending party that is responsible when they are shadowy ilk whose identity is nebulous or they hide behind bad laws and are rarely held legally accountable for the social outrages they wreak.

In such a case, you may elect to employ light while doing spellwork. Instead of using comforting candlelight, this would be the time to shine a dazzling LED flashlight on their picture, their name, or the business card of the agency they command or, if you lack such targeting information, on a scroll that describes the injustice in detail.

Visually blast them with such light in your mind. See them cowering in a corner, unable to hide from being exposed to the light of day.

Grant them no shielding, no quarter, and no escape from your glaring magical spotlight.

Your magical defense will encourage people to scrutinize them, conclude that their actions are despicable, and duly withdraw any support for them personally as well as for the policies they represent.

Using light magically can reveal secrets, lies, and the origin of, and motivation behind scuttlebutt and *clish-ma-claver* (a Witch word meaning rumor-mongering).

In the same vein, blasting an issue with heat during a ritual impresses others with a sense of urgency to resolve a problem, inspires clarity and certainty in how best to counter injustice, and instills trust in being able to magically succeed despite supposedly insurmountable odds.

Heat applied magically can constrict evildoers in a straitjacket of burning shame that forces them to act more positively, spike a spanking fever in the coldhearted that inclines them toward compassion, or instantly show the God/desses the intensity of your ire about the matter.

The tool you use will vary with the situation and your intention, but could include the following:

* A sun-heated pane of glass.

* A heated burin,[52] boline,[53] or similar knife pressed atop someone's picture, poppet, or other representation.

* A heated fireplace poker.

* A mirror lit by a light source.

* An electric space heater.

* Camping-type packets that heat up when you snap them.

* Heated metal trivets.

* Coins heated by the sun on your windowsill.

* Peppery herbs or spices that you ingest, feel their burn, and then turn the feeling outward toward your spell target.

* Stones that heat up when held in the hands.

* Sunlit prisms

Working fire magic requires more finesse than using either light or heat: It is tricky, mercurial. Learning fire principles is a key component in mastering the Element and working safe, effective fire magic. One of five building blocks (along

---

52 "Burin" (burr-en) is the Witch word for a sharp object used to bigrave a candle, a wax poppet, and the like. It can be as simple as a slim finishing nail that you drive headfirst into a recycled wine cork (the latter used as a wee handle), a wood-handled awl, or a stitch ripper used by those who sew.
53 "Boline" (boh-leen) is the Witch word for our traditional white-handled utility knife that is used for scraping wax and bigraving candles and wax poppets—everything except casting circle and calling the Quarters: We use a black-handled athamé knife to create sacred space in this fashion.

with Air/atmosphere, Earth/matter, Water/liquids, and Spirit/animating soul stuff), fire flies and makes tinder of treetops. Try to quantify it in dry BTU[54] terms, and fire will rebel by thwarting extinguishment.

Clients of mine who make mega-money digging trenches to try to contain wild-fires feel guilty for gouging the Goddess because they feel it is the equivalent of ripping out veins to break a fever. They oft feel frustrated by the frequent futility of the primitive fire-containing method. Indeed, in many ways this brutality is silly because the much easier and more effective way to forfend flames is to foster forests and wetlands and not introduce invasive species as the conquistadores did with the dry grass seed that feeds rapacious fires in Western states today.

Oxygen fuels fire's expansion. Our natural instinct when we espy a fire indoors is to open a door or window to air out the place or escape. However, this is often the wrong tack because the invisible gas we breathe rushes in and can make the fire spread. Instead, it's best to drop low and try to attack the fire from its base by using an extinguisher or to douse or smother it according to the combustion's composition. Witches' magical candlesnuffer tool works on this principle of dousing a flame by starving it of the oxygen that it needs to burn.

Fire lulls, seems to delight in thwarting assumption. Stray sparks easily smolder until they rage. Fire seeks to manifest: Linseed oil, wiring, hot computers, outlets, aerosols, paints, stains, home chemicals, lithium batteries—even building materials can combust spontaneously when the ambient temperature exceeds a certain degree (an increasingly common phenomenon in this time of global warming).

If you're interested in learning how to swallow fire, read the 2011 Kindle eBook titled *Fire Eating: A Manual of Instruction* by Benjamin "Garth" Mack and Brandon McKinney. Another book that features tricks and stunts is *Fire Magic* by Clettis V. Musson, originally a Brownstone Classic published in 1952, and reprinted in 2007 by Wildside Press.

Regardless of your bravery, always use reasonable safety protocols when you are working fire magic:

HONOR YOUR INSTINCTS: If you know in your bones that the weather's been too dry, spurn the expedient thing of erecting torches to welcome folk to your Samhain rite. You don't need an official "red-flag/don't burn" notice to exercise your Witchy common sense here; you know well enough that the slightest night

---

54 British thermal units, the measurement degree of heat that burning material produces.

breeze could waft brittle leaves into their flames, set your site ablaze, and ruin all your well-laid Sabbat plans.

If you assume that you should burn black candles at Samhain in honor of the Pagan Beloved Dead, remember how you regretted it last time: You spent weeks scraping the drips off of your lovely wood dining table only to discover that their splatter had irrevocably stained the piece. Instead, perhaps you should opt to light white candles whose color magically corresponds with spirits and ghosts.

If you've become used to routinely lighting a wood or isopropyl alcohol/Epsom salts—based fire in an iron cauldron but want to shake things up and evoke emotional poignancy, follow your heart. Instead, fill it with water and light floating candles atop it to represent Those Who Have Gone Before.

Mirror the Element or oppose it as you feel God-led. For instance, layer *types* of heat in the same spellworking, from weak to intense (typically no more than three at a time). Or mix cold-fire and hot-fire ritual elements, such as an outdoor starlit rite surrounded by electric BlissLights® or Star Shower® lights and a lit balefire circle focus.

WORK MURPHY'S MAGIC: Keeping in mind Murphy's Law ("If it *can* go wrong, it *will* go wrong), be a Wise Witch and exercise the Cardinal Virtue of prudence at all times.

Devise and hone backup plans for your backup plans. Learn how to do things before you need to use the skill; for instance, practice curing burns before you may need to help yourself or others. Make the skin/burn balm recipe I provide in *The Goodly Spellbook*. Memorize the "Three Ladies" burn-cooling chant and fever-breaking Abracadabra spells given there so that you can recite them with ease when the need arises.

Learn from *TGS* which stones invoke the sensation of "coolness," such as blue chalcedony, and which make a person feel "hot," such as carnelian, which, if used in spellwork, would tend to aggravate a bad burn rather than speed its healing.

Avoid using silver sulphadiazine on burns, which can evoke an allergic reaction in some folks. Instead, use natural tea tree oil to prevent a burn from getting infected, clean spiderwebbing to close a weeping wound, and sterile pressure dressings to reduce swelling; liberally rub hemp oil on the closed wound to speed healing and prevent scarring.

PLACE A CERAMIC OR CLAY TILE BENEATH EACH CENSER THAT YOU USE TO BURN INCENSE OR SPELL SCROLLS IN: Ceramic and fired clay dissipate heat and wood and metal tiles conduct heat, making these materials a less desirable choice to use beneath censers.

HOPE FOR THE BEST, BUT PREPARE FOR THE WORST: If you're using fire while conducting a large public gathering, pack and bring a well-stocked first aid kit. Put it in a central location and use it if someone gets burned. Don't worry about the cost of replacing what you use: Heal the injured person and replace the medical materials later.

Often, dancers at gatherings will walk straight into a lit tiki torch, but since most Pagan dances are fast-paced hand-to-hand affairs, they usually keep right on going and don't suffer any ill effects.

However, folks around a balefire for an extended period can get dehydrated and suffer dry, puffy eyes and superficial sunburn-like symptoms the next morning. Prevent dehydration by providing water, eye drops, and soothing skin lotion.

The final fire principle you need know is that fire is patient and opportunistic. I can't tell you at how many gatherings I've heard moanin' in the morning from people who dried their drums by the coals only to discover they had been rent asunder by the radiant heat of a rock-banked balefire.

For every cautionary tale, there are eons of success stories and every reason that you should master the power of fire. Although it is no more powerful an Element than Earth, Air, Water, and Spirit, it be mighty, mighty all right, so work well with it.

FIRE SUPERSTITIONS AND TABOOS

For most, the word "superstition" has negative connotations these days except among Witches. Scholars have discovered that there is often truth in the most seemingly outlandish ancient tale or myth, and Witches believe this to be true of superstitions as well.

Many superstitions display a certain logic and reasonableness. Today's superstition becomes tomorrow's custom, and Pagans prize honoring tradition and seeing connections in supposedly random occurrences. We might not believe *every* superstition, but we generally don't dismiss out of hand the wisdom they may possess.

Some Witches collect proverbs, mottos, and—you guessed it—superstitions. As we develop magical specialties, we deem it meet to collect superstitions about them. For example, one of my specialties is weather-sacting, or weather-working; therefore, I oft refer to rhyming couplet superstitions about weather phenomenon such as "Cover your mirrors and hide your shears when Zeus appears" (e.g., when it's lightning adoors) and "Red sky at night, sailor's delight; red sky at morning, sailors take warning." These superstitions are truly valid: I've *seen* lightning cease by observing the former exhortation, and checking the color of sky *invariably* correctly predicts sunshine or rain.

So consider the merit of these words of wisdom: No country on Earth lacks superstitions about fire.

* Leave a candle burning unattended and invite the death of a loved one. If you don't burn a candle to honor someone's passing, that person will become a hungry ghost desirous of offerings, propitiation, or vengeance.

* A fire that roars up the chimney portends strife or storm.

* Chimney sparks foretell important impending news.

* Raining fireplace soot presages disaster or bad weather.

* Putting log irons in a fireplace averts owl hoot that portends death or ill luck.

* Throwing salt, hot peppers, or vinegar into the fire will give an ill-luck hooting owl a sore tongue.

* Elizabethan-era folk believed that spitting into a fire conferred luck. This is probably a way to ameliorate the wrath of a despotic despot, for as all our kind know, "water puts the fire out."

* Carrying a bit of coal in your pocket confers luck. Witches oft use jet stone (polished rough coal): It's smooth, warm, and black in honor of our Ancestors. You can pick it off the ground on many a Blue Ridge Mountains walking trail.

* At midnight on mundane New Year's, Brits practice the custom of "first footings" to conjure 12 months of luck: They hold a piece of coal while visiting and wishing well to their neighbors.

* A cat sitting with its back toward a fire portends a hard frost or a long harsh winter.

* Driving livestock over cold Litha balefire ashes prevents cattle plague.

* Scarlet ladybugs[55] are associated with fire but can bring luck if they land on your clothing and especially on your hand. To ensure this, say:

---

55 Red-winged versus orange.

"LADYBIRD, LADYBIRD, FLY AWAY HOME.
YOUR HOUSE IS ON FIRE AND YOUR CHILDREN ARE GONE."

This is a protective, sweet sentiment to thank them for their largesse in deigning to bless you with trust.

* Swallow species of birds that nest on your roof or property protect it from storm and fire damage.

* The Japanese believe that tossing nail parings into a fire makes it vengeful and desirous to burn the tosser or the tosser's home; that tossing in persimmon pits causes leprosy; and that having red flowers in the house attracts fire.

* The Japanese so fear and loath *hinoeuma*—the year of the fire horse which occurs every 60 years—that women have been known to abort[56] if they get pregnant during that time.

* Tossing a bandage into a fire causes the wound to fester, burn, and heal slowly at best, and sets up scarring.

* Romanian and Turkish superstition contends that kids who play with fire will wet their beds.

* Ancient Romans contended that it was bad luck to mention a fire during a banquet; if you did, the only remedy was to spill water on the table intentionally.[57]

* British folk in the Midlands believe that if the fire burns brighter after being poked, it means that an absent loved one is in goodly spirits.

* The Welsh contend that a grave follows the appearance of a "hollow" in a fire. A hollow is when a log burns an "eye-hole" through its pith so that you can see the fire burning from inside its outer bark shell: hypnotizing when scryed, but a baneful portent of friends' and family members' mortality.

* Coffin-shaped coals that fly out of a fire portend death; coal cradles are an omen of an imminent pregnancy.

* The household will have bad luck if ash embers aren't removed before bedtime.

---

56 Not that Pagans prohibit abortion, for we believe that since all souls reincarnate, every fetus that isn't born for diverse reasons—whether it be due to spontaneous body expulsion caused by physical issues, or the host's free will—if it is its compulsion or task to reincarnate on a particular time line or planet, it will simply seek out a body until it is reborn.
57 Water puts fire out; that is why Witches can cast circle and/or then anoint Initiates using salt water first, and then cense the sacred space or participant with incense.

* The Scottish believed that they would have ill luck all year if they didn't burn a fire the entire night of the New Year. This magical blowback from the person's unmitigated gall in ignoring the tradition also attached to anyone who later dared lend that person a coal to try to relight the home fire.

* If fire burns to one side, it foretells a wedding.

* If a fire suddenly roars, it portends a visit from a stranger.

* People in Kentucky believe that it's bad luck to burn bones.

* It's unlucky to have two people kindle a single fire.

* A spitting, roaring fire portends an argument.

* Sparks foretell a letter coming or predict that a maiden's suitor will visit.

* A fire that burns blue means that spirits are present.

* Poking a fire you haven't made yourself is unlucky.

* If a log or coal rolls away from a fire, name it after the person whom you want to come visit you, and then spit on it: They'll arrive promptly.

* It is unlucky to turn a log over in the fire; leave a fire be.

* If a fire pops, stir it to prevent argument.

* If fire pops at you, avert the death or ill luck that will follow by tossing salt on the fire.

* A fire that dies out before consuming all the fuel is unlucky.

* If lightning strikes a tree, put the fire out with milk, not water.

* Burning lightning-struck wood attracts death in the family.

* Dreaming of fire portends good *and* bad—an unexpected windfall of cash, news, bad luck, family problems, an impending argument, and looming illness.

* If you dream of fire out of season,[58] you'll be angry for no reason.

* To dream of smoke portends trouble or death.

As does each of the other four Elements, fire has its own traditional *taboos*. Beyond mere superstition, magical practitioners should observe and honor these customs:

---

58 Before or after summer, or Beltane to Mabon.

Don't personally light a flame for which you don't take personal responsibility. If you think the flame or fire is polluted with ungoodly ingredients, extinguish it and replace it with more pure ingredients. Never blow out a flame. Instead, extinguish it by smothering it, putting ashes atop it, or with a snuffer.

SPIRITS OF FIRE: ELEMENTALS, ENTITIES, AND DEITIES

Compared with the spirits associated with the other Elements, fire Spirits have been singled out for special derision and have been used for centuries by ceremonial magicians who compelled them to serve their needs. Fire is prized only when it is controlled, for example, to melt steel; it is roundly reviled when it "breaks out."

Fire Spirits have received blistering human disparagement—the worship of this fire Spirit suppressed by a long-forgotten conqueror, solar deity's virtues radically changed in an attempt to fuel fervor for war.

Monarchs often conflated fire Spirits' names,[59] which confused their subjects and strengthened royal power, and they adopted and discarded fiery names at whim to conform to changing political trends. One day a fire deity might be revered; the next day it might fall out of favor following fire-and-brimstone denigration by Popes and preachers.

Despite these vicissitudes, Pagans retain our appreciation for fire and the Spirits, entities, and deities associated with it. We know fire as animated—a conscious Element similar to ourselves—as capable of brilliance as of burning bridges.

Witches use magical correspondences to attract, prevent, and appease fire. We strive to cultivate fire as a friend rather than approach it as a foe to be feared.

FIRE ELEMENTALS

An Elemental is the most primal expression of the Element of which it's composed. Fire Elementals are entities that embody light, heat, and dynamism. They existed long before humans evolved and seem to take little notice of us whereas we are ever entranced by their antics.

---

59 Witches began going by a magical name centuries ago to prevent us from revealing the identity of fellow Crafters while we were being tortured: Pru Proctor would be quickly captured and burned to death, but the Witchfinders couldn't prove who "River" or "Reed" was—it could be anybody: man, woman, or child. We retain this tradition today so that the Craft community can ensure that we act ethically, which is why Pagans new to the Path shouldn't choose names that many people associate with magic, such as Merlin, Morgan Le Fay, and Raven. Be original in your choice of a magical name so that you can earn a reputation unique to you that can't be confused with any other in Wiccandom. However, don't pick a fiery name because you could easily end up embodying its destructive aspects.

You can summon Fire Elementals by working with sharp objects, blades, scissors, swords, and the like. You can mollify, mitigate, or negate one of them by countering it with the Element *opposite* it in nature. For instance, if lightning threatens to split your home in twain, becalm it by offering pre-saved frozen hail in the watery Western direction.

The Witch name for Fire Elementals is "salamanders." They are depicted as white lizards (as in white-hot fire), and indeed, dancing flames resemble the fast-darting slitherers for which they're named. Many medieval grimoires include detailed illustrations of these magical creatures. They look more fat than the typical slim reptile lizards that we see in forests. Some drawings show them with four legs and feet, and some depict them as more snake-like, *sans* appendages.

The following is a non-exhaustive list of fire Elementals that illustrate how ubiquitous they are worldwide. Feel free to research, discover, and work magic with any, all, or others of these as you please. Throughout these lists "/" indicates name equivalents or different spellings of the same name.

* HESTIA—The firstborn daughter of the Grecian Goddess Rhea and God Kronos (Time), Hestia is the Goddess of the hearth.[60] She keeps the home fires burning and promotes domestic contentment. Often conflated with Vesta (see below).

* NOTOS/NOTUS/NODUS—Mentioned in Virgil's *Aeneid*, a South wind that blows toward the North direction. The Spirit of hot, moving air, Notus can be destructive and is associated with knots.[61]

* SALAMANDER—Spelled Salamandra in Verso Col. IV *The Demotic Magical Papyrus of London and Leiden*[62] and described as "a small lizard which is of the colour of chrysolite. It has no feet." Described by the medieval alchemist-author Paracelsus as a being that lives in fire and can withstand high temperatures. Known in British Gardnerian Witchcraft as a white or red newt that wriggles amid flames, Salamanders are associated with the South Quarter direction. These magical creatures are ascribed the ability to extinguish fire. Live wetland salamanders emerge when a damp log they live in is tossed into a fire.

---

60 Called "the domus" in other Nordic-European cultures.
61 Witches long sold seafarers magical cords to knot to dispel a gale or to untie to conjure a sail full of wind when they were foundering in the doldrums.
62 By F. Ll. Griffith, published by H. Grevel and Co., London, 1904. A collection of ancient Persian-Greco-Roman spells found, translated, and used by some Witches today. Indeed, we included many from a similar source in *The Goodly Spellbook: Olde Spells for Modern Problems*.

* **VESTA**—A feminine fire Elemental oft wrongly considered a Goddess. Spirit spawn of the ancient Greek Titan Earth Goddess Gaia and the Time God Kronos.[63] Vesta was not originally depicted in human form. She is associated with the concepts of flow and ease. Ovid wrote that she requires no offering effigy. Later, Virgil wrote that she was more easily felt than explainable. Now she is considered the animating spirit of eternal flames. Barefoot mothers and matrons annually honor Her by ritually dousing their fires on March 1 and rekindling them to bake hearth-bread offerings. Vestalia is June 9 in the Gregorian calendar.

FIRE ENTITIES

Intermediate beings with power and sentience above those of primal Elementals, yet beneath those of deities, these entities can assume diverse forms ranging from mythological animals or monsters to personifications of concepts and demigods. Unlike fire Elementals, entities interact with humans and can aid us if they feel inclined, or harass us if it suits their mood.[64]

---

63 Variously spelled Khronos, Kronus, Kronous, Chronus, and Chronous.
64 Some fire entities are sexually dominant, such as *incubi* and *succubi* (male and female fiery sex Spirits, respectively). These types are rapacious opportunists that prey on the lonely who pray to the Moon to send them a mate: The entity hears their desperation and becomes the person's Spirit lover—the best the person ever had—until the Spirit controls the person's life, pushes away all his or her friends and family, and often leaves the person in the gutter of degeneracy. An incubus or succubus singular rarely divulges its true name to its victim, but some are given in Leland's *Etruscan Roman Remains*. The way to dispel them is simple: Eat 15 peony seeds.

The following is an intriguing list of fire entities that you could magically work with during twilight, in the garden (deva), and during rituals and spellwork:

* Ao—The Maori personification of daylight.

* Camilla—"Fiery one," an ancient Italian queen who fought invading Trojans bare-breasted. Invoke Her for audacious strength and protection.

* Cherufe—A gigantic Chilean male monster that dwells in volcanoes and is composed of molten lead. Cherufe is attributed the source of volcanic eruptions and earthquakes, and is believed to be able to swallow young women whole.

* Chimera—An ancient Anatolian (Turkey) female creature that terrorizes. She is a winged serpent with three heads—one of a dragon, one of a goat, and one of a lion—whose mouths shoot flame.

* Dagr—The Nordic personification of daytime.

* Deva—Sanskrit, from the word meaning "a being of brilliant light." A generic term for fairy-like Spirits of nature, gardens, flowers, and storms.

* Djinn/Jinn—Fiery or blue genii[65] that emit no smoke. First written of in ancient Araby, this class of entity predates humans. Capricious and kindly in turn, djinn live for thousands of years, instantaneously traverse vast distances, and are able to possess people or aid those whom the desert renders desperate.[66]

Legend has it that female djinn abide in a glass bottle, and male djinn live inside a lamp. Once released from their confine, they are somehow magically bound to grant three wishes and only three wishes: to become a higher being, kill an enemy, and allow more than three demands (e.g., granting an infinite number of desires). In mythoi, this gives rise to the most typical and shrewd request to enslave the genie to accomplish trivial manual tasks or convenient commands.

* Dragon—A flying, scaly reptilian with bat-like wings, sharp teeth, and talons on its four feet that flames prey or enemies with fire from its mouth. Chinese dragons have serpentine bodies and no wings; their method of flying remains a mystery.

---

65 Plural, from the ancient Greek word *genos*, meaning "race, stock, kin, kind." Now genus oft is paired with species in the classifications of plants.
66 In a typical Pagan dichotomy, the dune djinn seem similar to the mermaids of the sea waves that sailors experience, who sometimes sing or drag them to the depths, or occasionally swim them to the surface.

Dragons are venerated as being communicative and intellectually superior to humans. European dragons were demonized as being malevolent and were equated with Satan and Paganism. Many myths maintain that dragons live in caves and guard treasure (e.g., magical secrets). These days they are oft heard flying on the winds whistling around mountains.

* FIREBIRD—A brilliantly plumed Russian entity. Waving a single one of its gorgeous feathers can illuminate a dark room. Armenians contend that its song rejuvenates the land. A firebird can verbally negotiate with humans and blesses those who treat it kindly but dooms all who dare to try to capture and exploit it.

The phoenix is a type of a firebird. The ancient Persian birdlike creature Simurgh may have been the original firebird, and ancient astronaut theorists contend that its carved imagery described early humans' experiences with aliens from another planet, with its wings being their spacecraft.

Phoenixes sport vibrant plumage, and their cry is pleasant. These magical birds are associated with the wisdom born of longevity because each lives 500 years before shedding and using its feathers to make a funeral pyre nest. They then spontaneously combust and reconstitute themselves from their ashes.

* FIRE GIANTS—Large, tall, wise, humanlike Nordic creatures with claws, fangs, and a shock of bright orange hair, fire giants live in mountainous regions in groups of two to five. They live upward of 350 years. When threatened, they use their body heat to explode rocks and rain them down on the enemy.

* HESPERUS—Venus in Her guise as the star that shines brightly during eventide.

* KAPRE—A male nocturnal humanoid creature 8 to 9 feet tall with a hollow laugh. Kapre inhabits Philippine forest and mountain areas. While his camouflaging invisibility belt enables him to prank travelers, he mainly focuses on attracting females by smoking a perfume-filled pipe.

* LUCIFER—Initially a name for the morning and evening star Venus,[67] the female Lucifer was reclassified as masculine, and Her merits were demonized by monotheists who deemed her Yahweh's primary antagonist. Her original female aspects remain in appellations such as "light-bringer" and "day-star."

---

67 Refer to the Venus entity Hesperus above.

* TAMA-NUI-TE-RA—The Maori personification of the Sun.

* WILL-O'-THE-WISP—Also called a "corpse candle," a "fetch candle," and "ghost lights" because their individual and group appearance is believed to be an omen of death. "Mysterious light which hovers in the air and moves away from you if you follow it,"[68] Will-o'-the-Wisps are actually a species of fairy whose body is a colored orb.[69] They populate remote forests and mountainous terrain,[70] and often move about as a clan.

If you're intrepid, Wisp orbs may appear at your campsite's periphery at night, and if you earn their trust by acting quietly respectful in the forest, they may even bring their young to show them what humans look like.

Will-O'-the-Wisps' ethereal sentience entice many to try to follow them, but don't do it—they may beckon, but will remain elusive. You could easily end up being fairy-led into a mushroom fairy ring and never be seen again.

Wisps can be protective, however: Several saved my life and that of two Covenmates when we got stranded and had to stand all night with our backpacks pressed against a perilously high mountainside. Sympathetic to our plight, they entertained us until sunrise, when we were able to escape danger by carefully walking out on a path no wider than a single foot fall at a time.

* XIUHLCOATL (Sheeool-*kohtl*)—An Aztec fire serpent manifestation of the solar heat and the fire God Xiuhtecuhtli (Sheeoo-*tekoot*-lee). He has a long, serpentine-segmented body, an upturned snout, and two feathered heads—one representing the land, and the other, natural disasters. This sky dragon issues fire from his fanged mouth.

* ZHULONG—A Chinese daylight dragon.

* ZORYA UTRENNYAYA—One of two daughters of the Slavic Sun God Dažbog. Zorya U. personifies the morning star that enables sunrise (e.g., Venus).

* ZORYA VECHERNYAYA—Another daughter of the Slavic Sun God Dažbog, Zorya V. personifies the evening star associated with sunset (Venus again).

---

68 Richard Cavendish, *Man, Myth and Magic: An Illustrated Encyclopedia of the Supernatural*, Vol. 14, BPC Publishing Ltd./Petty and Sons Ltd., Leeds and London, 1970.
69 White, blue, green, and red. White and blue are beneficent, but if they glow green, they're thirsty, and if red, they are parched and angry, so use a water hose to moisten their area or erect a birdbath or a similar water source.
70 An example of the Will-o'-the-Wisp are the famous mysterious Brown Mountain Lights in western North Carolina.

The following is a specific set of fire and light Spirit-entities listed in ancient Mediterranean spells and printed as the collection *The Demotic Magical Papyrus.*[71]

The name meanings provide clues to the many magical ways you could invoke their aid, such as to enable invisibility, to dazzle an attacker so that you can escape, to extend a fire, to spotlight yourself in a crowd, and more. My favorites are Light Master PEPPER PREPEMPIPI and Fire-Whirler PYRICHIBOOSELV.

Spelling of these terms is as it appears in the *Papyrus.*

* AIO—Light-Forcer.

* ARARRACHES—Ra-Horus (of the Two Horizons).

* AREI EIKITA—Light-Giver, Fire-Sower.

* AZAI, AION, and ACHBA—Beautiful Light.

* BEEGENETEE—Glory-Light.

* ELOYRE—Fire-Delighter.

* GALLABALBA—Fire-Driver.

* HEKATE—Torch-bearer, torch-carrying.

* LAO—Eternal sun; Fire-Feeler.

* OAI—Light-Breather.

* OE LAO EEEAPH—The One who holds the power of fire.

* OXY—Brightly.

* PENTITEROYNI—Fire-Walker.

* PEPPER PREPEMPIPI—Light Master.

* PHNOYENIOCH—Fire-Body.

* PROPROPHEGGE—Primal Brightener; Bright Lightener.

* PSYRINPHEY—Fire-Breather.

* PYRICHIBOOSELV—Fire-Whirler.

---

[71] Not demonic but demotic, as in popular, of the (ancient) common people; simplified ancient hieratic Egyptian writing between 700 B.C.E. and 500 C.E. Source: www.dictionary.com/browse/demotic.

* SANCHEROB—Light-Mover.

* SEMESILAM/SEMESEILAM—Light-Maker/the God who illuminates . . . the world.

* SITAMESRO—Figure of the Sun.

* SOYSINEPHIEN—Firelight-Increaser.

* SOYSINEPHI ARENBARAZEI MARMARENTEY—Firelight Maintainer.

FIRE DEITIES

Pagan cultures worldwide revere the most wise, rarefied, powerful, and magical beings: Gods and Goddesses. The big bangs that create the multiverses are assumed to be white-hot happenings. Human survival often depends on our ability to start a fire in bleak weather conditions. Artistic inspiration is oft described as a "feverish" obsession, and doomsday scenarios typically predict a planet-wide conflagration.

It should come as no surprise then that thousands of fire deities exist in every culture as far back as human life goes; and that it pays to respect their powers, mythoi, offering preferences, and so forth. Cultivate the beneficence of God/desses associated with fire.

Fiery God/desses are associated with volcanoes, lightning, the Sun, stars, light, day, noon, summer, the South, rage, the hearth, deserts, metallurgy, hot winds, thermal springs, love and war, and similar things.

Their attributes are perpetuated from generation to generation in the recitation, reenactment, and publication of their mythoi—stories recounting their origin, land where they've been traditionally worshipped, and their affinities and magical exploits. Pagans appease Sun Gods to forfend drought and propitiate them to attract vigor and willpower.

Familiar names abound, such as Ares, Belonna, Mars, Durga, and Thor, but there are also fascinating names such as Cit Chac Coh and Kakupacat (Mayan) and Zababa (Mesopotamian).

Read and reference books that list Pagan deities according to their magical mythoi associations. Some of these tomes that relate their exploits are inexpensive, such as *Gods, Demigods, and Demons: An Encyclopedia of Greek Mythology* by Bernard Evslin; others are gender-specific, such as *The Book of Goddesses and Heroines* by Patricia

Monaghan; and still others are inclusive and multicultural, such as *Encyclopedia of Gods: Over 2,500 Deities of the World* by Michael Jordan.

As with many magical life form names, you can't always assume by the way an Elemental, entity, or deity's name is spelled that a particular deity is masculine, feminine, androgynous, or asexual by nature. For example, because each country ascribes different names to the same deity, sometimes rather counterintuitively, names ending in "a" or "e" are actually masculine in the way their bearers act, manifest, or are described. Often, neither the beginning nor the end letter reveals an automatic relation to the being's gender or the amount of intense magical "juice" that They can grant to fuel your spellwork.

Although these deities sport different names in different cultures and timelines, They manifest similar powers. They are the apotheosis[72] of heat and fire.

Imploring a deity always adds extra power to rites and spells when that deity agrees that your cause is just and your intention is well-meaning: Invoking *more* than one whose attributes support each other and your purpose further increases your efforts' potency and the efficacy of the spell's outcome. Beyond giving deities offerings They prefer, you can garner Their ongoing aid by purchasing a calendar listing Their feast days and making merry in Their honor in creative ways.

The following is a list of dazzling deities. Get to know these deities' abilities, attributes, backgrounds, and virtues. Invoke Their aid and beneficence in Sun worship rites and fire spells to improve your, others', and the planet's health, stamina, and vigor.

Pray to Them in thought, and extol Their merits aloud in circle with epithet-descriptions such as "All-Seeing Sun-Disc," "He Who Shines Exceeding Bright," or "Dark Moon Goddess Who Yet Illuminates the Night."

Summon, conjure, and honor fire deities. Share Their effect on your life with family and friends, and you'll continue to benefit from Their largesse.

* AETNA—Many cultures equate fire and mountains with Goddesses: the Element Fire because of women's ability to gestate life and the geography because of women's endurance. Akin to the Hawaiian volcano Goddess Pele and the Japanese Fuji, Aetna was the original Roman personification of the Italian volcano Mount Etna.

---

72 Epitome: the utmost powerful example, characterization, or expression of a concept or thing.

* AGNI—A Hindi God of Sun, fire, and sacrifice.[73]

* AH KIN—A Mayan Sun God Who protects against night harm.

* ÁINE—An Irish Goddess[74] associated with hot months and the Pagan Litha Sabbat (summer solstice).

* AION—A fiery aerial Gnostic agathos daimon (good spirit) described as a "fire-breathing god" in A. Dietrich's 1903 book *Eine Mithrasliturgie.*[75]

* AKYCHa—An Alaskan Inuit solar deity.

* ALAUNUS—A healing Sun god of the Gauls who imparts the power of prophecy.

* ALBINA—An Etruscan Italian dawn Goddess who protects star-crossed lovers.

* ALECTRONA—A Grecian Sun Goddess associated with waking in the morning.

* AMATERASU—A Japanese Sun Goddess.

* AMUN/AMUN-RE/AMUN-RA/AMMON/AMEN—The chief Egyptian-Nubian deity who dispenses fertility and justice, protects travelers, calms stormy seas, forgives the contrite, and shows mercy to the wretched.

Amun's sacred stone is the fossilized spiral-shelled cephalopod called ammonite because it resembles the ram horns the deity wears on His head.[76] Alexander the Great considered himself divine after an oracle declared him "the son of Amun." When a grimoire spell specifies "the semen of Ammon" as an ingredient, it means the herb houseleek.

* ANYANWU—A Sun-dwelling God of the African Igbo people.

* APET—The Egyptian creatrix, "mother of fire."

* APOLLO—A Greco-Roman light and Sun God who dwells on Mount Olympus.

---

73 Ancient Pagans often sacrificed animals or even humans to solar deities not because they were primitive and cruel but rather because these represented the highest caliber of offering they could provide the God/desses they revered. Pagans still seek to give the Gods the best tangible offerings we can afford, but also count our personal sacrifices made while mastering and practicing magic throughout our lives, such as exercising patience and tenacity in prevailing against persecution, championing peace in a war-torn world, and so forth.

74 Reference the fire, volcano, and summer Goddess categories in *The New Book of Goddesses and Heroines,* Patricia Monaghan, E. P. Dutton Publishing Co. Inc., 1981.

75 For more information on Aion, read the spell "To Conjure a Helper Spirit," *The Goodly Spellbook,* 2014 edition.

76 First depicted on Amun iconography and statues after the Egyptians conquered the Kushites, whose chief ram-like deity they identified with their own chief deity, Amun.

* ARINNA—A Hittite Sun Goddess.

* ARYAMAN—A Hindu Sun God.

* ATANUA—A dawn Goddess of the Marquesa Islands folk.

* ATARAPA—A Polynesian dawn Goddess.

* ATEN—An Egyptian Sun God depicted as a solar disc with flanking wings. His singular worship by the devotee pharaoh Akhenaton in opposition to Pagan tradition unleashed the precedent of monotheism on the planet.

* ATUM—An Egyptian God of the sunset.

* BALDR—A Nordic light God.

* BEIWE—A Sami Goddess of sun, spring, and sanity.

* BELENOS—A Gaulic Sun God.

* BHRIDE/BRIGANDIA/BRIDGET—"The bright One," a healing Irish fire Goddess associated with cauldrons and goldsmiths.

* CH'ASKA—The Incan Venus, Goddess of dawn and twilight.

* CHU JUNG—A Chinese fire God.

* CHUP KAMUI—An Ainu Moon Goddess who swapped places with Her brother (probably the Sun) to become a solar Goddess.

* DA-BOG—A Slavic Sun God and the father of sunrise and the sunset entities Zorya Utrennyaya and Zorya Vechernyaya described earlier in this book.

* DOUMU—A Chinese Sun Goddess occasionally conflated with the Buddhist deity Marici (see below).

* EKHI—A protective Sun Goddess of the Basque.

* ELAGABAL—His name briefly appended to that of Sol Invictus (see below) when the Roman Emperor Elagabalus[77] unsuccessfully attempted to unify the Pagan and Judeo-Christian faiths, this Syrian Sun God could easily have become the God that everyone worships today.

---

77 Also known as Heliogalabus, Elagabalus ruled for four brief years from 218 to 222 C.E. until Praetorian guards assassinated him for having attempted to elevate himself above the God Zeus/Jupiter.

* ENDOVELICUS—A Lusitanian solar *and* chthonic[78] God.

* EOS—A Grecian Titan dawn Goddess.

* ÉTAÍN—An Irish Sun Goddess.

* FERONIA—A reclusive woodland-dwelling Italian fire Goddess associated with fertility, thermal springs, volcanoes, and Earth's molten core. Her feast day is November 15.

* FREYR—A Nordic God associated with sunlight.

* GABIJA—A Lithuanian fire Goddess who can be summoned by tossing salt atop a consecrated flame.

* GERRA—A Babylonian/Akkadian fire God and successor of Gibil (see below), later conflated with the God Nergal.

* GIBIL—The Mesopotamian fire God, predecessor of Gerra.

* GNOWEE—An Australian Aboriginal[79] solar Goddess who searches daily for Her son (probably the Moon); the Sun Herself, as well as symbolizing the forlorn torchlight She uses.

* GRANNUS—A Celtic Sun God Who empowers thermal spring spas.

* GUN ANA—A Turkish solar Goddess.

* HASTSEZINI—*Hast* means "deity" in the Native American Navajo tongue, so His name is actually Sezini. The inventor of fire, depicted as burning cedar wood.

* HECATE—Originally the ancient Egytian frog Goddess Hekt. Later Hellenized as Hecate. The Greeks insisted that She was the first female deity in their pantheon and credited Her with issuing Fate from her hip.

Hecate is a triple Goddess with three distinct manifestations: a flirtatious virgin maiden, a fertile nurturing mother, and a wise magical crone. Statues show all three guises standing in a round, with all six hands holding a traditional Witch implement such as a "knife of midwifery" to cut a babe's umbilical cord (an athamé), or depict Her as a single figure holding a lit torch aloft in each hand. Hecate used these torches to light Demeter's way in the Underworld to rescue Her daughter Persephone from Hades.

---

78 An underworld afterlife deity.
79 Interestingly, all Australian Aboriginal solar deities are Goddesses.

Hecate rules land, sea, and sky; considering Her association with torches, by extension, she also rules volcanoes, hot springs, hot stars, and the Sun.

* **Helios**—A Grecian Titan Sun God. When a grimoire spell calls for "the semen of Helios" as a component, it means the herb white hellebore.

* **Hemera**—A Greek Goddess of the day; the female personification of daylight.

* **Hephaestus**—An Etruscan Italian/Greco-Roman Olympian God mentioned in the ancient *Iliad*, *Odyssey*, and *Theogony*. Hephaestus is lame and is considered the father of metallurgists and blacksmiths. He is a maker of magical tools. When a grimoire spell specifies as an ingredient "the blood of Hephaistos," it means the herb wormwood; if it requires "the semen of Hephaistos," it means the herb fleabane.

* **Hestia**—Depicted in female form, Hestia succeeded the Roman Elemental eternal flame Vesta described earlier in this book. Associated with the Lares (ancestral spirits who protected the household).

Hestia is a pretty Greek fire Goddess who takes the form of a small burning fire tucked inside a wall niche that maidens and/or slaves tended in each household and that family members propitiated with offerings and libations.

Six-year-old white-clad girls served as Her temple priestesses for 30 years[80] and, if adjudged guilty of violating their virginal vows, were punished by being buried alive.

When a grimoire spell necessitates "the blood of Hestia," it means the herb chamomile.

* **Hino-kagu-tsuchi**—A Shinto fire God Whose birth killed the Goddess Izanami, from Whose spirit-corpse sprang eight thunder Gods.

* **Ho-musubi-no-kami**—*Kami* is Shinto for "deity," so this God's name is actually Ho-musubi-no: He Who protects humans against fire by igniting one using only a stick and board.

* **Hors**—A Slavic Sun God.

---

80 A cycle of service that balanced their practice of purity because dark, heavy, slow Saturn completes an orbit around the Sun every 30 years.

* HORUS—An Egyptian raptor God Whose left eye is the Moon and whose right orb is the Sun. Son of the sibling deities the Goddess Isis and the God Osiris.

* HUEHUETEOTL—An Aztec fire God.

* HYPERION—A Grecian Titan light God.

* INTA—An Aztec Sun God.

* INTI—The Sun God, primary deity of the Inca.

* ISTANU—A Hittite Sun God associated with blistering judgment (i.e., justice/vengeance).

* ISUM—A benevolent Babylonian/Akkadian fire God.

* IXCOZAUHQUI—A paternal fire God with the appellation "yellow face in the house."

* KHEPER/KHEPRI—An Egyptian God of sunrise depicted as a scarab beetle, a symbol of rebirth.

* KHNUM—An Egyptian sunset God and counterpart of Khepri.

* KINICH AHAU—A Sun God of the Maya.

* KOYASH—A Sun God of the Turks.

* KUPALO—A midsummer Goddess of Russians and Balkans yearly worshipped by ritual balefire leaping. Devotees depicted Her as a straw effigy, anointed Her with river water, and then set Her adrift to take away the troubles of the village.

* LO'CIN-PO'GIL—The South Siberian apotheosis of fire, His name means "owner of fire."

* MAGEC—An African light and Sun God worshipped by the Tenerife tribe.

* MAHUIKEZ—A Tunga Polynesian fire God associated with volcanic earthquakes.

* MAIA—Origin of the name for the month of May, She was initially a Grecian night sky Goddess who later was revered by the Romans as a generative fire deity similar to Feronia.

* MALAKBEL—An Arabian Sun God.

* MALINA—A Sun Goddess of the Inuit in Greenland.

* MARICI—A Buddhist Goddess of light, the Sun, and the heavens (i.e., the sky and stars).

* MASAYA—An oracular Nicaraguan crone Goddess associated with volcanoes.

* MAWU—An African solar and lunar Goddess revered by the Dahomey people.

* ME'MDEYE-ECI'E—"Father Fire," a benevolent Eastern Siberian sky God.

* MERI—A Brazilian Sun God.

* MITRA—A Hindu God of morning sunshine.

* MITHRA—A Persian light God; successor of Phanes and associated with Sol Invictus (see below). Particularly worshipped by Roman soldiers.

* MOLECH/MOLOCH—An Egyptian African kinglike fire God of the ancient Ammonite tribe.

* MULITTA/MYLITTA—Also called Afka after the name of Her sacred spring, She is a Persian Goddess Whose flowing waters are peppered by heavenly fire.[81] In antiquity, priestesses of Mulitta offered their tresses in honor of Her and had sex with all comers to Her sacred grove. Similar in sexual connotation to Venus and Aphrodite.

* NAHUNDI—A Persian Sun God associated with the law (i.e., the light of truth versus the darkness of lies).

* NANAUATZIN—An Aztec Sun God.

* NETO—A Lusitanian solar deity.

* NIHA-TSU-HI-NO-KAMI—A Shinto God Who enables yard fires.

* NGAI—An African Sun God worshipped by the Kamba, Kikuyu, and Maasai people.

* OLWEN—A beautiful Welsh maiden Goddess associated with light and the Sun; the name means "white footprint."

* OYA—A nine-headed Brazilian Goddess of the Macumba people, She rules fire, is depicted holding flame, and is married to the lightning God Chango; worshipped by practitioners of Santeria.

---

81 Symbolizing sex or impregnation or a spring beside an active volcano.

* PERASIA—A Cappadocian Goddess Who enables her priestesses to walk through sacred fires unharmed. Similar to the war Goddess Artemis.

* PHANES—The Grecian progenitor of light and life later associated with the Persian-Roman light God Mithra. Depicted as gold wings surrounded by zodiacal symbols.

* PROMETHEUS—Greek, "forethought" (brother, Epimethius, "afterthought"); creator of humanity and opponent of Zeus, He gave mortals fire. Rescued from Zeus's wrath by the hero Heracles.

* PTAH—An Egyptian God Who represents the invisible Sun at night.

* RA/RE—An Egyptian Sun God; the Goddess Isis absorbed His power by employing cunning magical arts.

* RAVI—A Hindu Sun God.

* SARANYU—A Hindu Goddess of daybreak.

* SAULÉ—A Baltic Sun goddess Who imparts fertility.

* SAVITR—A Hindi God Who rules the rising and setting Sun.

* SEKHMET—An Egyptian lioness Sun Goddess Who creates and roams deserts. She is bloodthirsty and difficult to appease or slake once She sets Her course on vengeance.

* SHAMASH—An Akkadian Sun God of justice; the male equivalent of Shapash (see below).

* SHAPASH—A Canaanite Sun Goddess.

* SOL INDIGES—Latin, "indigenous Sun." An ancient eighth century B.C.E. solar God ubiquitous for His many suffix appellations throughout Roman antiquity, such as Sol Invictus.

* SOL INVICTUS—Latin, "invincible Sun." The official solar God of the later Roman Empire, particularly revered by the military. Depicted wearing a torso shield shaped like an eagle (the messenger entity-familiar He used to communicate with humans) and wearing the same nimbus crown of sharp, radiating Sun rays as America's Lady Liberty statue.

Although he is often honored in August, many scholars contend that His feast day, December 25, inspired Christians to claim it as Jesus's birthday.[82]

* SÓL/SUNNA—A Germanic solar Goddess.

* SOPDU—The Egyptian Sun God of scorching summer heat.

* SULIS—A Roman healing solar Goddess worshipped at the thermal spring spas in Bath, England.

* SURYA—A Hindi Sun God.

* SVAROZIC—Similar to Prometheus, this Slavic Sun God gave humanity fire. He rules marriage and metalworkers such as jewelers and weapon makers.

* TABITI—An ancient Scythian Goddess Who protects animals from fire. Conflated with Vesta/Hestia and later worshipped by Russians.

* TATEVALI—Huichol Meso-American, meaning "our grandfather"; a shamanic[83] fire God associated with red cardinal birds.

* TEOYAOMICQUI—An Aztec Sun God and psychopomp[84] Who rules the sixth hour after sunrise (i.e., noon).[85]

* THEIA—A Grecian Titan Sun Goddess.

* THESAN—An Etruscan Italian dawn creatrix Goddess similar to Albina. She is associated with new life, birth, and reincarnation.

* TOHIL—A Mayan God of sunrise and lightning.

* USIL—The Etruscan Italian equivalent of the solar God Helios.

* UTU—A Sumerian Sun God of justice similar to Shamash.

* VERBTI—An Albanian fire God associated with the North wind and later demonized.

---

82 Ancient monotheists honored death days (Ecclesiastes 7:1) because they hoped the deceased resided in heaven, and because they believed that people were born sinners, they railed against the temptation of overimbibing when celebrating birthdays. (Sources: *Against Apion*, II.26, Josephus; *Homilies on Leviticus*, VIII.3.2, Origen.) Jesus's supposed birth was first observed in Alexandria on December 25, 432 c.e. Source: http://penelope.uchicago.edu/~grout/encyclopaedia_romana/calendar/invictus.html.
83 A shaman is the equivalent of a Witch, with the word "shamanic" meaning magic by trance, ecstatic dancing, and/or ingesting herbal entheogens (sacred psychedelic substances).
84 A death guide through the underworld/afterlife.
85 This number reflects the pre-Judaic six-pointed solar symbol called the Star of David.

* VULCANUS—A Roman God of forge fire similar to Hephaestus. His annual honorific is the Vulcanalia rite during high Italian summer on August 23.

* WALA—An Australian Aboriginal solar Goddess.

* WI—A Native American Lakota Sun God.

* WURIUPRANILI—An Australian Aboriginal solar Goddess similar to Gnowee. She uses the Sun as Her torchlight.

* YHI—An Australian Aboriginal Sun creatrix Goddess of light worshipped by the Karraur people.

* XIHE—A Chinese Goddess Whose Sun chariot is powered by dragons.

* YUYI—A Chinese Sun God.

* ZUN—The African Zuni name for the Sun and origin of the tribe's name.

ACCRUING FIRE-STARTER STOCK

Prepare to work sultry magic by steadily recycling and collecting inexpensive and indispensable fire accoutrements and tools.

Keep a journal to log your fire magic acquisitions and keep a running list that details what you lack or want and in which you can track your fire spell results. This can be a simple spiral notebook, a write-it-yourself book, or an intricately tooled leather blank journal from a source such as Gaelsong.®

Fire can rise and fall unpredictably and smoke can smolder or reignite unexpectedly, so have the following on hand to contain, start, and douse a fire.

FIRE CONTAINERS

* BRICKS, CERAMIC, OR MARBLE TILES AND TRIVETS—Set a burning censer, magic lamp, or pillar candle atop the fire container to diffuse its heat and reduce the risk of spreading fire or burn-scarring table surfaces.

* CENSERS—This ritual fire tool comes in an almost infinite variety of shapes, sizes, colors, and materials—particularly ceramic, heavy tempered glass, iron, copper, silver plate, brass, pewter, and carved stone such as agate or soapstone.

Some types of wood resist heat, but I don't recommend wood censers inlaid with bits of decorative brass. If you feel compelled to use wood, put a slab of it beneath your censer for added fire protection, although in my experience it tends to increase the odds of the censer slipping.

Traditional censers are shaped like bowls, and Witches typically fill them with dry sand or dirt to stanch bottom-glowing embers and add stabilizing weight to the censer to minimize tipping and the scattering of the flame.

Many censers come with a removable wire grate lid on which the coal and incense burn or between its slots to vertically slip a stick of incense to burn down into the self-smothering filler sand. These *static* censers are rarely moved from their initial placement but can be moved by hand to a different location when they are cool to the touch.

Other censers come with chains attached to enable you to hang them from the ceiling or swing them by hand and infuse ritual participants or a sacred space with billows of scented smoke through motion. Their metal sports cutouts in shapes such as crescents and five-pointed stars to allow airflow to keep the fire stoked.

Use natural items as a censer. Fill a shell or geode with sand or dirt to burn cone incense on or fill a nutshell halfway with sand or dirt to burn a small stick of incense in.

Make a censer by wrapping a clear, lidless glass jar's upper threads with a long length of arts-and-crafts wire or yarn and form a handhold/hanger. Decorate the glass by using a permanent ink marker or paint. Use tongs to put a lit piece of charcoal in it, top with resin incense, and swing the censer rhythmically by its hanger frontward and backward while making a processional or casting circle.

* CLEAR GLASS JARS—Label and store chunk or powdered resin or dried herbs in these jars to burn as incense or to toss in a balefire by the handful. You can also use them for the following:

  1. Keep fragile saltpeter-impregnated charcoal discs in them to burn incense atop.

  2. Transport lighters, matches, pyrotechnic powders, or dousing water to outdoor gatherings or rituals in them.

  3. Collect ash remains from magical fires in them for use as an ingredient in future spells.

  4. Store blank paper scrolls in them to inscribe and burn in spells.

5. Keep small birthday candles in them in Elemental colors for use in quick spells, one-time prayers, and so on.

6. Put wax tea lights or battery-operated tea lights in them to serve as a magical tabletop lamp or ritual room Quarter altar decor. Swirl the wax melt to paint their insides in wicked and evocative ways. (*Witch tip:* Dripping red food coloring into melted white wax makes it resemble spooky blood or drips.)

7. In lieu of lit jack-o'-lanterns, bid your ritual participants to progress through your town holding battery-operated tea lights in jars.

8. Store fire-conjuring charms, fire-quenching talismans, and fiery-scented essential oils in glass jars or vials.

9. Use a wax tea light in a baby-food jar and screw on the lid for safe transport. Unscrew it to burn in a tent while, say, camping at a gathering and then screw the top back on to starve the flame of oxygen when you're ready for sleep.

* IRON CAULDRONS, FROM FIST-SIZE TO HUGE—Fill with sand or dirt and use as an incense censer. In lieu of a stone-lined fire pit adoors, use as a balefire container. Brew potions or boil Sabbat feasts in them.

Too poor to afford a large iron cauldron to use for fire leaping wish magic? A less expensive option is a half of a round barbecue grill.

Use an outdoor "chillum" firebox in lieu of a fire pit or dig a fire pit in your backyard or forest circling site and then line it with stones.

* METAL COOKIE TINS—These come in myriad metallic designs, are stackable for storage, and are good to keep wax tea lights, cone incense, and *katharmata*[86] in that you want to burn later as an offering to the Goddess Hecate.

* PLASTIC FREEZER BAGS—Keep ritual parchment paper in these to prevent it from getting damp and curling before you can inscribe and burn it during spellwork.

* TALL CERAMIC, RUBBER-GASKET-SEALED, METAL-LATCHED CONTAINERS— Often used to store grain, ground coffee, or dried beans, these provide excellent

---

86 Ritual remains such as leftover unburned candle bits.

storage for stick incense, packaged stacks of ritual charcoal, long fireplace matches, and the like.

FIRE STARTERS

* A FLINT AND A STEEL SLAB OR A KNIFE—Place fine kindling shavings in a shallow depression dug in the ground or on a nonflammable surface such as concrete. Strike the steel with your flint or strike a flint with a knife until sparks ignite the tinder.

* BIRTHDAY CANDLES—These diminutive candles are inexpensive, are portable, come in Quarter colors, and are readily available in grocery stores. Or you can quickly achieve a trance state by vertically setting a birthday candle in melted wax in the bottom of a silver chalice, leaning over the brim, and staring intently at the pulsating flame. Or you can burn finger-size "chime" candles whose heat propels Yuletide aluminum angels around in carousel fashion. Or you can burn short, white emergency candles that come in packs for use during power outages.

* CHARCOAL—Magical charcoal is about one-third the size of a typical barbeque briquette and often has a shallow dip on top to serve as a reservoir base on which to burn resin (dried hard or gummy sap) incense. It often comes in packs stacked one atop the other in silver metallic wrapping. Each is impregnated with saltpeter or a similar granular flammable to speed its ignition. Use ice cube–type tongs to hold a charcoal's sides while patiently lighting it by candle flame until it glows red.

* DRIED TEA, HERBS, AND FLOWER PETALS—These make goodly fire tinder or incense when put atop burning charcoal.

* "FATWOOD"—Some folk buy dense strips of plastic packaged wood to use as a fire starter. Fatwood is designed to light fast, but I've never found it easy or useful fire tinder.

* FLOATING CANDLES—Come in a wide variety of sizes, shapes, and colors, especially discs and roses.

Create an impressive focus by lighting and then placing these atop the water in an outdoor pool, grotto, or water feature or fill a cauldron with water and make a floating lit arrangement of them in the center of your magic circle.

I once lit hundreds in Asheville's downtown reflection pool in front of our tall obelisk. The random candlelight was beautiful and touching as my Samhain Sabbat participants circled around it while chanting at night.

* FLOATING WICKS—A piece of wick about ¹/₂ inch (1.27cm) long that you push into a clear plastic roundel lightweight enough to float atop oil. These come in packs of 25 to 100 or so. They are a goodly inexpensive way to make a Witchy tabletop arrangement for Sabbat celebrations. Buy clear glass votive holders or elevated champagne or dessert glasses from your local charity resale shop. Fill with olive oil, float the wick, light, and enjoy the reflections.

* HIMALAYAN ROCK SALT, PUNGENT HERBS SOAKED IN UNSCENTED MINERAL OIL. MOSSES, SCENTED CANDLE SHAVINGS, LOAMY GRAVEYARD DIRT—Any or all of these and other substances can be put in a glass diffuser to emit the particular aroma that you want in order to evoke specific feelings in visitors, students, or others.

* JOSS STICKS—Long, thin pieces of wood used to light candles or incense. Substitute inexpensive wooden kebab skewers sold in a pack in the grocery store or make something similar from recycled chopsticks or spindly debarked twigs. Keep dry for use in a clear plastic sandwich bag.

* LAMPS—Magical lamps come in diverse forms: colored glass lit by votive, taper, or pillar candles inside; electric models that change their light into Elemental colors; lamps shaded with sheer capiz shells; colored portable kerosene-fueled lamps—the sky's the limit. These can be magically worked and can also serve as a fire source in a pinch.

Create your own ancient-style clay oil lamp. Finger-sculpt clay into a ¹/₈-inch (3mm)-thick hollow, fist-sized round with the top sliced off. Poke a hole larger than your wick on one side and roll out an Aladdin-style lamp spout and attach it to the outside of the hole. Use a sharp stylus or straw to impress designs on the outside. Get the lamp fire-cured by a local potter. Pour olive oil in the lamp's reservoir, snake your wick through the spout so that it extends ¹/₈ to ¹/₄ inch (3mm to 6mm) past the spout opening, and immerse the opposite end of the wick in the oil inside the lamp. Light and enjoy your magical handiwork!

* LIQUOR—Create an affecting ambience by pouring moonshine or other clear flammable spirits such as gin and tequila into a leakproof glass container and setting the top of the liquid alight.

You can use a stained glass–like vase, a small clear mixing bowl, or a glass mortar that you muddle herbs in—even teensy shot glasses. Just don't fill to the brim or let it overflow or spill.

* MAGNESIUM STRIKER—A ¼-inch-thick rectangular silver metallic piece about 3 inches long that often comes with a drilled hole on one end with which to attach to a keychain or carabiner onto a backpack or belt-loop. You can shave the metal with a knife to produce shavings to add atop gossamer fire-starter flotsam. The flammable bits gently alight and their power stoke a "not happening" fire attempt into a rager in no time.

* MATCHES, LIGHTER, LONG-BARRELED FIREPLACE LIGHTER, PROPANE KITCHEN TORCH, AND SMALL GAS CAMPING COOKING SETUP—Between uses, keep survival matches or a lighter in a plastic baggie or waterproof container while backpacking or stored in a damp basement ritual room. Also consider buying a long-barreled lighter for fireplace logs to light ritual candles with. These prevent finger singe.

In my backpack I carry a silver refillable Zippo® lighter with the Witch sentiment "Blessed Be" engraved on it in flowing script, to forfend burns and to enable life-saving fire starting.

When you are camping during Pagan gatherings or outdoor Coven Sabbats, a small propane kitchen torch can help you light a fire during inclement weather, and a small screw-on gas canister setup will quickly boil a meal in a pot of water. Both are portable and cost-effective fire starters.

* OILS—For thousands of years the ancients immersed braided fiber wicks (often cotton) in olive oil inside a fired clay lamp, and burned the flammable liquid to illuminate sacred rites.

The scent that burning oil emits depends on its purity or the chemicals or additives that it contains. For example, burning mineral oil may smell metallic and an artificially scented nonessential oil may emit a noxious odor depending on what the maker used to blend it.

* OIL DIFFUSERS—Witches often prefer organic scent methods to buying chemical-based air freshener sprays made by companies such as Glade® and Febreze.®

Like candles, decorative oil diffusers come in diverse shapes and materials. Some are molded resin and thus weather-resistant and good for outdoor use. Others are more delicate glass and metal models intended to burn indoors.

Some oil diffusers work by the principle of absorption and evaporation and may be ceramic vase-like vessels filled with thin hollow reeds that wick up scented oil. They require no flame to burn and release a scent into the air over time.

I often soak wooden skewers available at the grocery store in scented oil and put them in a chalice or container surrounded by votive candles. This is a much cheaper alternative to buying the expensive scented "reed" sets that have become popular.

Instead of directly setting oil ablaze and risking burning down my Covenstead, I often gently infuse my environment with scented oil by warming it in a shallow glass dish in an iron holder by using a lit votive candle beneath the diffuser. You can also put shredded scented dryer sheets into a diffuser that you don't light; their scent can help repel bugs during the summer!

Other kinds of oil diffuser sport a convex glass saucer to pour essential oil into. Their oil is warmed gently and released into the atmosphere by a tea light set below it.

Still others are inexpensive circular ceramic diffusers with the upper half of the roundel removed. The diffuser is balanced atop a light bulb and oil added to the inside of the "cup-up" circle by the dropperful.

Oil diffusers are a great way to combine scent with fire and artistic beauty. I enjoy working with them because they allow infinite creative options depending on the season or Sabbat.

For example, during the Yule holidays I often substitute pure essential oil with dried bayberries, cloves, citrus rind, and cinnamon sticks with a touch of oil to help extract their scents over time. During the dog days of summer when the heat is oppressive, I put small seashells in a clear martini glass and douse them with sea-scented essential oil.

* PAPER—Paper bags, packing paper, plain white printing paper, and so on. Avoid starting a fire with newsprint or gift wrapping, as these materials contain color chemicals that will off-gas an obnoxious odor. Don't waste your precious costly parchment to start a fire: It's meant to be burned after having been inscribed with a spell, with a fire already roaring to waft your wish to the attention of the God/desses.

If you are burning adoors or near a draft, use aluminum foil to shield a fledgling fire from wind.

* RESINS—Resins are plant and tree saps that are sold in dry lumps, "tears," pulverized powder, and a sticky-gummy form in a plastic pouch. Amber, myrrh, copal (pine sap), frankincense, patchouli, and other resins are flammable when lit and stay lit when atop a burning coal—often longer than their leafy counterparts.

For portability and to save storage space, you can pulverize resin by putting it inside a paper bag and beating it with a rubber mallet. Keep the powder dry in a clear labeled and dated glass jar.

* SALTPETER—Also called niter, this combustible white powder is potassium nitrate (KNO_3)—a natural mineral and alkali metal salt of potassium ($K+$) and nitrate ions (NO_3) that is a good source of nitrogen. It is used to make incense and charcoal light easily and burn evenly. It is available at pharmacies and from online occult suppliers. Keep it dry in a screw-top stash can or plastic bag between uses.

* STICK, CORD, AND FLAT BOARD—Hand-dig a small ground depression and fill it with a cone of wood or bark shavings or similar combustible ephemera. Wrap two horizontal sticks together at their ends in an infinity pattern and then wrap them together in a loose spiral. Sprinkle more ephemera in the middle of the stick board above the depression. Vertically insert atop this the sharpened end of a burn-hardened stick and then loop another cord midline around it. Tie each end of this cord onto a separate wood stick bent bow-like away from you and beside your vertical stick.

Use one hand to saw the wood part of the bow back and forth to twist the vertical fire-starter stick and the other hand to stabilize the bottom of the fire-starter stick, until smoke and embers form. Transfer the embers to the shavings and gradually build a stronger fire.

Make this setup in advance and carry it when you hike adoors or keep it in your car trunk in case you break down and need lifesaving heat. Store it dry in plastic wrap or bags.

* VASELINE®-SATURATED COTTON BALLS—Prepare this waterproof fire starter in advance of camping. Thoroughly knead Vaseline into several separate cotton balls. Melt a previously burned candle in a double-boiler setup on a stove burner. Use disposable chopsticks to fish out wicks (discard) and individually dip and fully saturate each ball in the liquid wax. Place the balls atop aluminum foil and freeze solid dry. Label and store in a container ready to pack for camping adoors. As needed, select as many balls as you think you need to start a fire in windy and rainy conditions. Knife or split them in twain. Remove and finely fluff the fiber. Light.

* WAXED WICKS—These days one can hardly be sure what a wick's composed of. It could be utterly synthetic, chemically treated, or metal-infused and thus, may barely resemble its fiber precursor.

The best natural waxen light-primed wick materials are composed of a single type of fiber or braided/woven fiber strands of the following:

1. WOOL—sacred to Earth. Burns fast; can spread sparks.

2. HEMP—sacred to Earth. Burns strong and long evenly.

3. COTTON—sacred to Air. Burns quickly, leaving copious ash.

4. JUTE—sacred to Fire. Burns slowly, but prone to smolder.

5. BAMBOO—sacred to Water. Hard to light, but snuffs itself.

Since the advent of electricity, the populations of developed countries have largely chosen to discard the knowledge of how to safely burn candles, oils, and fire and hence tend to view combustibles from a base of fear as being the "eternal enemy."

* WOOD—During early spring, collect the deadwood that fell on your property or in your neighborhood during winter winds, ice storms, and snows. Glean wood that neighbors discard after trimming trees around the home or tree refuse left behind by construction workers building a new development.

Saw limbs and break sticks over your knee to fit your fireplace, iron stove, or outdoor fire pit or to transport in your backpack to start a campfire. Stack and dry the wood horizontally to minimize bowing and burn it as desired instead of paying for the delivery of a truckload or cord of expensive hardwood.

Because wood is an endangered fire source, Witches prize its magical applications and effects. For example, Coven Oldenwilde has a huge outdoor food smoker.

We use various varieties of dried wood kindling to slowly infuse our feast foods with sweet spring and summer flavors such as apple and peach and savory fall and winter flavors such as black cherry and hickory.

We select wood to burn to support our ritual and spell intentions. We heed fires—hearken to the quality and timing of their pop, sizzle, and roar—and scry them intently for the shapes their flames and embers form to get insight into, and omens of, present situations and forewarning of events to come.

FIRE DOUSERS

Witches burn a lot of candles and work many kinds of fire magic, but we don't relish getting burned or having our Covenstead go up in smoke, and so we learn the best ways to prevent unwanted fires and to douse them when needed.

Learn the rules for stopping different types of fire, such as those involving flammable gases, plastics, oils, candle wax, electrical equipment, and so forth. Sometimes you should douse fire with water or flour, sometimes you should smother it, and at other times, other means avail. For example, it's preferable to smother-snuff a candle rather than blow it out or spritz it with water: Blowing out a candle insults the spirit of the Element; when it feels baited or dismissed, it can react by expressing its ire in the form of flash fires, electrical glitches, and the melting of objects that are flame-resistant.

Be conservative with what you put near tall taper candles. Window curtains, magical oils, herbs, and other Witch accoutrements can easily be set alight.

Keep a bowl of water in the West Quarter. I have a large oval wall mirror hung horizontally there, and a taper melted a portion of its silver plastic frame; it would have consumed the entire Covenstead had I not used the Western water bowl to swiftly put it out. Here are ways to put out a fire:

* BUCKETS AND CARAFES—Fill buckets with sand, dirt, or water and toss their contents onto fires to smother or quench them.

* Normally you wouldn't burn a candle unattended, but there are many spells that actually call for this or for burning a spell candle over several days. One way to do this safely is to film it burning and use a smartphone to check on it periodically.

* Beware confusing a recycled carafe that you fill with white wine to imbibe during the after-spellwork Cakes & Wine ceremony with one filled with isopropyl alcohol that you use as the flammable liquid for making a cauldron fire.

* White wine and isopropyl resemble each other in candlelight, and you wouldn't want to try to douse a fire with the former or accidentally drink the latter. If you commonly eschew a plastic container for ritual room liquids in favor of using glass wine carafes, label their ingredients to ensure that everyone in circle knows what is in them and doesn't accidentally reach for the wrong thing during a fire panic should the fire extinguisher malfunction.

* CANDLESNUFFER—Acquire a metal candlesnuffer (a bell shape on one end and a straight handle on the other). Silver preferred, but brass ones abound. Keep the snuffer atop your Eastern or Northern main altar. Use the magical tool to suffocate candle flame after spellworking.

If you lack a candlesnuffer, put out stick incense by grasping its nonburning base, turning it upside down, and burying the lit end in the sand.

You can also clap candle flame out using both hands, or use your thumb and forefinger to pinch it out if you're not afeared (a Witch word for courageous) or have "asbestos hands"—those resistant to fire like the kind that many chefs cultivate over time.

* FIRE EXTINGUISHERS—Keep an extinguisher near the South Quarter altar in your ritual room and master how to use it prior to need. Keep another in the kitchen and wherever else you feel the need.

A member of your local fire department will inspect your fire extinguishers' efficacy for free, and one or more are often required if you conduct large public gatherings on city-owned parkland. Anyone who hosts a gathering should have several on hand to protect participants.

Install a smoke detector away from door and window drafts on each level of your home, particularly in places ripe for fire, such as your kitchen, utility room, workshop, attic, and basement. In America, twice annually check and/or replace the batteries when Daylight Savings Time changes (i.e., when you're told to "spring forward" or "fall back" one clock hour).

SMOKE MAGIC: INCENSE AND FLAME SCRYING RITES

S moke hangs in the air, coalesces, swirls, floats, reaches skyward, obscures with a haze, assumes the scent of its combustion source, inspires romance and conviviality, and reinforces emotional and familial bonds. Smoke escapes, dissipates, and seeps into objects; it is difficult for mundanes to contain and direct its motion.

Herbal smoke contains particles that can be purposefully inhaled to induce a spiritually altered state. Witches sometimes do this via a "cape huddle" in which we sit surrounding an iron cauldron with dried, lit herbs inside it and cover ourselves with our cloaks and hoods to minimize the amount of smoke that escapes. We inhale until we feel its effects and then cast spells.

MAKING HERBAL INCENSE

Pagans' love of offering herbs and resin incenses to the Gods was one of the *driving raisons d'être* for the establishment and defense of ancient spice trade routes that some credit with the spread of "civilization."

Even today nothing evokes the feeling that magic's afoot as much as a comforting cloud of irresistibly scented resin incense a-bubbling-melting atop a glowing orange coal set atop sand in an altar censer.

Incense serves as a silent cue for Witches to center our thoughts and feelings, to focus on and excitedly anticipate the wondrous spellwork about to occur. It reminds us of previous rites we've enjoyed and unites us with the long, unbroken line of Pagans who have burned incense for eons to summon, commune with, appeal to, thank, and appease the Gods.

Incenses can smell intoxicating (opium), alluring (patchouli), sexy (musk), stimulating (dragon's blood), refreshing (sage, lemongrass), inspiring (Nag Champa®), comforting (sweetgrass), pungent (mugwort), and repugnant (asafetida). All have their appropriate spellwork uses, and burning them is a way to add yet another layer of magic to help you get your needs met, just as you layer proper ritual timing, color, candle, garb, decor, and spell ingredients into a synergistic whole designed to accomplish your magical goal.

Traditional incenses come in raw resin form that resembles lightweight pebbles or small stones, aromatic powdered woods, and dried herbs, and I recommend that you use all of these at some point or another. To prepare resin incense, put the amount you plan to use in a plastic grocery store–type bag or inside a paper bag and then crush it to powder with a rubber mallet or hammer. Remove the powder and store it in a labeled, dated glass jar or something similar. Witches often put the pulverized powder atop a lit charcoal by using a teensy silvery spoon.

Modern incense typically comes in tall stick or conical form and may be pristine, such as hand-rolled Japanese rosewood sticks, or composed wholly of artificial chemicals designed to merely simulate a scent.

Always break off the weak, raw wood end of stick incense so that each piece you set in a censer will stand safely upright. The weak end is so fragile that it has a tendency to tilt the stick and make it fall and make things smolder or catch ablaze.

Some folks find that after protracted use of cheap incense, they develop an allergy to the additives that manifests as a wicked headache after spellwork. You can avoid this by using only "pure" incense or by arranging fresh herbs, flowers, or fruit that you like and can tolerate and changing them to suit seasonal changes.

If you choke on traditional incense, consider making and suspending from a ribbon an orange pricked with cloves and rolled in ground cinnamon. If you find, say, store-bought frankincense smells tinny or metallic, go adoors and scrape off pine tree sap, dry it in chunks, and crush and burn it instead. In this form, it is called copal and is one of the most ancient incenses on the planet.

MAKING INCENSE CENSERS

WINE BOTTLE CENSER

Wash and remove the label from a wine bottle, preferably one made of blue or green glass. This does double magical duty by keeping away the Evil Eye and curses from jealous neighbors.

Take a round silvery keychain ring and insert between its rounds an incense stick. Insert the incense upside down into the bottle and balance the key ring on its rim. When you're ready to burn some scent, grasp the top of the ring, lift the incense stick out of the bottle, light its bottom, let it catch alight, then reinsert it back into the bottle upside down.

These censers work well when placed on a windowsill. The incense smoke may discolor the bottle over time, so occasionally remove the ring/incense stick and wash the ashes out and the soot off the inside of the glass.

WINDOWSILL INCENSE BURNER

Make this by splitting a length of bamboo or river cane in twain along its length and using one or more segments horizontally. Use a burin to bore a hole near one end to hold the incense stick aloft above the wood. Decorate the cane if desired, but certainly stabilize its cup-up curve by filling it with gem chips or sand to prevent it from spilling its ashes sideways onto your sill.

SMOKE

Scry smoke every chance you get. Scry it in all forms that you make or that spontaneously manifest during spellwork. Scrying can be an intensely focused staring at a wisp, or it can be a smoke shape that is noted by other ritual participants or that you happen to catch out of the corner of your eye in passing during a circle.

Like all Elements and manifestations of the Elements, smoke is animate, living. The way it acts has meaning and can foretell boons or warn of setbacks to come of which you're unaware.

At first glance smoke seems utterly daunting to get to know. You cannot hold it; you can often barely take a picture of it. It blows, billows, disappears, regroups, elevates itself toward the ceiling, settles itself close to the ground, and envelops and obscures with impunity according to the rules of science and its own sensibility.

Humidity, barometric pressure, weather, wind direction and speed, topography, combustion type, matter consumed—all these factors affect the way smoke behaves. But smoke's sentience, its own unique life form, is what can make two identically set fires smoke differently and can give many a Pagan pause about how to understand and rightly interpret its mood and movement to our and others' benefit.

Thankfully, smoke works as do the other Elements, according to ancient, reliable magical correspondences: This means this, that means that, and there are reasons for everything that it does.

Here are some examples to help you begin getting to know the power of smoke:

* Smoke seems "Crazy-A-Maze"—Moves hither and thither, yet it actually moves in ways that forms magical symbols that Witches can readily recognize and interpret. Here are some examples:

A. Smoke rises = goodly circle ventilation; dry weather forecast. All's well.

B. Smoke settles = magical circle ventilation is inadequate; rain is coming. Open a window; keep an eye out for negative omens or ill luck.

C. Smoke tendrils upward = Power present: You're on the right track. If you can, make the flame spin fast.

D. Smoke tendrils curve downward = negativity imminent. If you can redirect the smoke upward with your mind, you're on the right path. If not, snuff smoke and scry again later.

E. Smoke tendrils spin deasil (sunwise/clockwise) = energy high; proceed with spellwork as planned.

F. Smoke tendrils spin widdershins (ayenward/counterclockwise) = It's a goodly omen if performing a banishing or repulsion spell. Otherwise, energy low; adjust spell plans to accommodate participant mood. Encourage brief expression of feelings; watch for warnings.

G. Smoke points *toward* a Quarter direction of your ritual circle setup or by extension, *away* from a Quarter: Use rational magical correspondences as explained and illustrated in *The Goodly Spellbook* to know their meanings.

H. North/Earth (opposite South/Fire Quarter) = Earth over ego. The Gods support you. Make a tool or use a hand-made magical ingredient during spellwork (think heavy substantial). Expect a tangible result of your spellwork.

I. East/Air (opposite West/Water Quarter) = Wits over will. The Gods know your issue; employ verbal magic. Win the debate about a matter by using logic, intellect, or inked spells, replete with Witches secret language words, magical alphabets, or numbers of squares, etc; during circle spell work..

SOUTH/FIRE (OPPOSITE THE NORTH/EARTH QUARTER) = Guts for glory. The Gods share your ire about an injustice issue. Work physical magic. Use movement, dance, or magical postures or gestures; play a musical instrument; or leap a cauldron, etc.

WEST/WATER (OPPOSITE THE EAST/AIR QUARTER) = Fuel with feeling. The Gods feel your pain. Use pathos magic. Cry, freak, scream, spit, stomp, tweak—be radical and intuitive. Sacrifice rare spell components, chant, dance or sing during spellwork.

Smoke forms magically symbolic shapes, letters, numbers, and pictures. Books abound listing the meanings of thousands of mystical symbols. These are not always the same as dream symbolism in which overindulging in ham can inspire a nightmare about pigs that bite back.

Thanks to the Internet, even though these magical symbols are ancient, even the most seemingly obscure can be tracked down in olde grimoires, medieval books about alchemy and celestial or ceremonial magic, Egyptian hieroglyphs and Homeric poetry or Nordic sagas, and similar places.

These universal symbols are common to cultures worldwide, and their multilayered depths of meanings are based on magical correspondences such as those illustrated and explained in *The Goodly Spellbook*.

Spirals, stars, circles, waves, dots, arrows, figures, eyes, and combinations of these strokes unite Pagans in an ongoing primal understanding of the natural forces that

affect life: how things work and how they can be thwarted, mitigated, or supported in a way that precedes and transcends the limitations of constantly changing norms and fads in languages.

Learn and appreciate as many symbols as you can, just as you would learn about deities you don't yet know well. Practice drawing them until you perfect the flourishes, for you will use them in innumerable magical ways.

As opposed to an intricate Asian mandala, simple magical symbols are a goodly meditative focus and an easy spell focus to draw and encourage participants to visualize. Comforting and inspiring, magical symbols enable Witches to aspire to ethical heights and increase our strength of will. They can serve as mental mottos to keep us on the Path during trying times.

Being smoke, it can feel daunting to get a handle on, But delight in its uniqueness *and* basic manner and you'll be able to understand its ability to communicate to you wisdom, warning, and insight on a par with more overt Elements such as Water and Flame.

Watch how smoke symbols change with the seasons, mutate as you mature, and alter depending on the caliber of your Covenmates.

Don't panic if smoke curls widdershins: This is not always negative, but it might actually mean that a troubling thing will soon abate or resolve as you desire.

Consider the movement of smoke in the context of the direction, intensity, or quirkiness of the smoke from other candles or fires burning at the same time and in the same sacred space.

If smoke makes you feel that it wants you to move to a different area in the circle, follow it. If it seems menacing, unstable, or agitated, prudently observe it from afar. Log, date, and track how it acted when you attempted this or that spellwork.

SMOKE SPELLS

SMOKE SENSATION SPELL

Learn the burn. With a Covenmate, partner, or friend you trust, face the South direction and don a blindfold.

Have the other person light different kinds of incense, herbs, and oils that you can burn during rites and smell and try to identify.

Speak your intuition aloud into a voice-activated tape recorder or have the other person write down your impressions.

Practice until you can readily differentiate the kind of smoke that dried herbs produce versus fresh; that expensive incense emits versus inexpensive; and that different oils produce—typically, darker in color and deeper in aroma than subtler white-gray herbal incense smoke.

SPEAKING WITH SMOKE SPELL

Treat smoke as you would an ephemeral ghost: Ask it direct questions and heed its response. Don't sell its sentience short; although silent, smoke speaks volumes.

Generally, a deasil spin is a "yes" answer and widdershins a "no," but there are nuances and exceptions to these givens as well. Practice makes perfect.

BOTTLED SMOKE SPELL

Save smoke in a recycled clear glass container and use it when you want to infuse a spell with extra power.

Label and date the contents to remind you why you chose to contain that particular kind of smoke. Did it help transport you to an ecstatic state during a ritual? Was it part of an inspiring Sabbat? Did it inspire a vision or epiphany? Did it presage positive change for you?

SMOKE SPIRIT-SUMMONING SPELL

A daimon is "the spirit or essence of a thing," long vilified by monotheists as being an evil "demon." Daimons are legion and unique: They are Entities below the Gods and above the Elementals in power, and they have unique mythos histories, magical names, epithets, associations, and powers.

Daimons pre-exist humans. Most are benevolent—well-meaning and enabling to humans—but a few are mercurial enough to avoid and grant a wide berth: They are impatient and find human stupidity intolerable.

Work with the goodly ones, such as healing Buer. Light a candle or fire and demand that they manifest in smoke form and communicate with you.

Sustained, strident demand is crucial: If it is confidently performed, the daimon will coalesce smoke into a human form or a symbolic form associated with its legendary powers. It may literally contrive a way to speak to you or otherwise telegraph its desires, abilities, and limitations.

Dismiss any effort by it to scare you with phantasmagoric images of itself: Instead, elicit from it specific vows to enable and champion you.

Conjure a smoke daimon by lighting a stick of incense inside a triangle drawn nearby, but apart from, the circle that you cast. Let naught breach either boundary: Once you and they are confined within your protected realms, you're both in them until your needs are met.

Lists of known daimons and drawings of what they purport to look like are in olde grimoires such as the *Renaissance-era, The Key of Solomon the King,* and *Etruscan Roman Remains* by Charles Godfrey Leland.

FOE CURL CURSE

The smell of smoke panics some folk and offends others. If your spell targets deserve unnerving, make them hypervigilant by attaching the scent to their body, clothes, jewelry, home, transportation, or workplace.

Use the fingers of your left hand to upwardly twist into a widdershins spiral the tall candlewick on a black taper candle. "Dress" (anoint) the wick with the juice of a noxious plant such as mugwort or coat it with a cool melted resin such as odoriferous asafetida. Light the candle using your left hand and then position it so that its smoke curls *deosil*.

See the person perpetually enveloped in a cataract haze cloud—a stink that puts off everyone that person knows and encounters—as invisible finger tendrils of soft smoke thwart his or her hard-heartedness.

LAMP MAGIC: MAKING AND SPELLING WITH WITCH LANTERNS

The earliest cultures used the Element Earth to approach or breach the Element Air—"star heaven"—by blending clay with water and finger-forming small containers, hardening them in the heat of ferocious fires, cooling the result, and then adding and lighting a flammable liquid to light their way to temples and to pray and offer appeals or thanks to the Gods.

Flammables such as oil, resin incense, and alcohol were necessary for survival on a number of fronts and thus were considered a precious sacrifice to the deities that people adored and on which their thrival depended.

By Sumerian times, reeds in decorated wall sconces lit doorway arches, huts, temples, and public thoroughfares. In gratitude for the largesse granted, ancient Egyptians decorated their lamps, torches, and sconce holders with precious metals and semiprecious stones.

By the antique Greek era, no home was considered proper or complete unless it included one red lamp inset in a niche prominent to its entrance. Typically, the matron of the house would light it afresh each morning and the daughter or a young female slave would tend it night and day until it was due for a refresh; the man of the house would oft use it magically, although this is the most that's recorded. Since men were most out to the Senate or baths or what have you, it's more likely that the women and slaves of the house appealed to the genii in the lamp more often than the master did.

Greeks faced their lamps to thank the God/desses for boons granted or to imprecate Lares[87] for largesse and to magically conjure spirits for their specific desires.

---

87 Ancestral household spirits.

Lamplight was crucial for security, productivity, and religious observations. Everyone viewed the vessels as similar to sacred statues animated with divinity, with the ability to move and direct and advise humans. Indeed, they used the tools as a spell component with which to work all manner of magic as the need arose.[88]

Although the Gods may seem normally invisible, lamps give people the ability to actually *see* a deity *move about* in a shelter that serves as a physical extension of Themselves. A lamp's "mouth" surrounding its wick "tongue" is able to communicate, answer questions, or predict future events to its mortal charges.

MAKING LAMPS

ANCIENT CLAY OLIVE OIL LAMPS

Archaeologists have unearthed and preserved thousands of lamps used for utilitarian and magical purposes from antiquity. The version that the poor used were typically made by potters using local clays; the wealthy often used thinly carved alabaster, agate, or other stones or metals with cutouts and with oil reservoirs inset within them. The crude common lamp versions resemble the *Aladdin* movie style—shallow, fist-size, or a bit larger, some with long, graceful wick spouts and others with a simple "U" push-out on which to drape a wick.

The ancients mostly used as wicks rolled strips of linen or papyrus or scrolled papyrus. They filled their lamps with oil—what they called "genuine" (probably olive oil), "Oasis" (probably palm oil), or vegetable, as described in Col. XXVIII.ii *The Demotic Magical Papyrus*.

MAKING AN ANCIENT OLIVE OIL CLAY MAGIC LAMP

You can make an ancient olive oil clay magic lamp by using self-hardening arts-and-crafts clay. Olive oil is preferable for its triple virtues of burning brightly, burning long, and emitting minimal smoke. Do the following:

Use a shallow bowl as a mold. Turn it upside down and cover its outside with clingy plastic wrap (tuck a bit in under rim all the way around). Set it onto a sheet of wax paper on a flat surface. Use a rolling pin or your hands to flatten the clay into a $\frac{1}{4}$ or $\frac{1}{3}$-inch (6mm or 4mm) thickness. Cover the wrapped bowl with it, wetting the clay as needed to enable full coverage and prevent cracking from dryness. If desired,

---

88 Ancient spells published in *The Greek Magical Papyri* insist that those who cast curses and other "tough" spells never use a red lamp, as these should be reserved solely for ancestor and God/dess worship.

use a toothpick or a similar sharp object to bigrave the clay with ancient magical symbols or to inscribe it with a wish in a magical alphabet.[89]

Finger-roll a hand handle in an ear shape and wet, taper, and attach each end vertically on the left side of the bowl. Air-dry the bowl bottom a tad and then flip the bowl rim upward. Opposite the handle, push out a U- or an O-shaped protuberance at the rim to hold the wick. Air-dry the vessel for days, preferably in a sunlit windowsill, and then remove the lamp from your template bowl and remove the cling wrap. Roll out or finger-form and attach a top for the lamp with a circle cutout in the middle that you'll use to pour the oil into the lamp. Air dry.

Consecrate for sacred use by holding the lamp in your right hand and anointing it with salt water and then passing it through incense smoke. To burn, pour some olive oil into the lamp and insert into it the bottom end of your wick; then lay the other end atop the U-shaped protuberance or snake it through an O-shaped one. Allow the wick to absorb the oil for about half an hour. Light the end of the wick in the protuberance, and the first few times you use the lamp, prudently observe for leaks or fire hazard; the lamp should work well, however. Replace the oil if it gets rancid or is depleted from burning.

MAKING NONFLAMMABLE LAVA LAMPS

If clay isn't your bailiwick or your lease or occupancy rules forbid burning anything where you abide, make a nonflammable "lava lamp."

Lava lamps are meditative and come in all colors, sizes, shapes, and materials. They are goodly useful to induce a trance and improve scrying and divination skills.

Either magically decorate the base of a regular lava lamp that you purchase or make one in your favorite color, one for each of the four Elemental colors, one in each of the colors of the rainbow, seven in the chakra colors, and so forth.

MAKING AN ALKA-SELTZER® TAB LAVA LAMP

INGREDIENTS: Mineral oil; water; food coloring; Alka-Seltzer tablet; a tall clear glass container

Half fill the container with mineral oil. Add water and the desired amount of food coloring. One by one, add small pieces of an Alka-Seltzer tablet (five or six from one tablet). Enjoy the visuals!

---

89 See "Magical Alphabets," page 195, *The Goodly Spellbook: Olde Spells for Modern Problems*, Lady Passion and *Diuvei, Sterling Publishing, 2005, 2014.

Other, far more intricate recipes, many featuring toxic chemicals and expensive lighted bases, are available for free online.

MAKING A WINE BOTTLE LAMP

You can make a wine bottle lamp by using an inexpensive conversion kit from an arts-and-crafts store. The kit contains a long wick and a fireproof ceramic roundel resembling a doughnut (with an opening in its center).

Soak the wick in olive oil. Pour some olive oil into a clean, empty recycled wine bottle. Insert the wick into the roundel so that some protrudes above it and then put it atop the wine bottle's neck opening. Light the top of the wick and enjoy.

The best part of this kind of lamplight is its amenability: If you don't want to buy a kit, finger-form a roundel from self-hardening clay or a metal ring: anything fireproof that can snug your wick upright. Highlight the coolness of an intricate absinthe label or a liquor bottle that comes in an interesting shape, such as with the head of a cat atop it.

Or you can change the color of the wine bottle to reflect seasonal Sabbat changes or decorate the outside of its glass with magical symbols or magical sentiments by using a permanent marker (silver works well).

MAKING A CLEAR GLASS PILLAR CANDLE GLOBE OR URN

Yet another magic lamp option begins with buying a large, clear glass pillar candle globe or urn, usually inset in a stabilizing iron or metal base. These come in diverse shapes and are goodly altar decor.

Paint the outside of the glass with stained glass arts-and-crafts stains or shapes such as autumn leaves for the Mabon Sabbat, a crescent moon for monthly Esbat meetings, and a spring sapling for Beltane. Let dry and then insert a pillar candle and light it.

MAKING OLDE CARVED VEGGIE LAMPS

Not all magical lamps have to be permanent. Carving vegetables into magical lamps has its virtues, such as when you want to leave them as an offering adoors or when you don't want to transport lamps back from an outdoor ritual or gathering. Simply carve these on site, and when you're done burning them, pitch them into the balefire or let them naturally decompose.

Cucumbers, potatoes, pumpkin, radishes, rutabaga, squash, tubers—all these vegetables and more can be cut out or carved to sport faces, sentiments writ in a magical alphabet, symbols, natural designs, animals, and the like, through which a battery or wax tea light glows.

Use a permanent ink marker to draw a design free-form on your vegetable and then use a safety kit or any sharp object you feel confident wielding to carve around areas that you want to leave "negative" or without organic material.

In the olden days folk would tie hemp rope handles around these and progress through the streets with them to mark all manner of occasions. Longer string allowed them to swing the portable lamplight in mockery of the monsignor who swung the incense in church or even to spin it around themselves while dancing.

Consider suspending some from the ceiling to illuminate your circling space with a ghostly romantic traditional ritual effect that will impress the participants.

EASY-TO-MAKE LIQUOR LAMPS

Pagans have been burning liquor for lamplight since the invention of beer. Priestesses burned liquor lamps in temples for eons because liquor was considered a pure spirit of light compared with sooty wood or sticky oil. Tallow and beeswax came much later, and petroleum-based candles long after them. All but an alcohol fire has its issues, be it creosote accumulation, melting and spattering all over everything, emitting noxious fumes, and being overly smoky.

Leakproof stained glass candleholders make the best kind. Pour in a bit of clear liquor that contains no flavor additives—plain vodka versus lemon-flavored vodka, for instance. Match the liquid and delight in the animated kind of light this medium emits.

Or make your own version: Experiment with decorating the outside of different shapes of clear glass containers by using stained glass stain or permanent marker—whatever you like to color the light that the liquor produces.

MAKING SCENTED ESSENTIAL OIL DIFFUSERS

These days, glass and metal lamps are available online and from paper catalogs and so forth and come in all four of the Quarter colors (red, blue, yellow, and green) to enable you to set one on each altar in your ritual space and work them magically as needed.

Similarly, diffusers for gently disseminating scented oil throughout your environment abound, many with cutouts in magical motifs such as stars, crescent moons, and spirals.

Some oil diffusers work by the principle of heat: The higher the temperature is, the more scent is released. These diffusers require a tea light or electricity to heat the oil and diffuse the scent notes. Other varieties work by the principle of passive gravity: Reed ends are immersed vertically in a container of oil, and the scent wicks upward and disperses into the ambient air over time.

You can use either kind or both kinds, and depending on their construction materials, they can be readily decorated to suit changing magical needs. Although painting the unglazed clay variety isn't recommended, as that would impede the absorption and release of the scent, making a few slight silver or copper embellishments to highlight the cutouts would be fine.

The easiest oil diffusers to make are ambient and passive; they require no heat source. An ambient diffuser can be as simple as making a shallow clay dish and pouring in an essential oil. Or you can repurpose a small dip bowl or a tiny bowl for cleaning your fingers in at the table and add drops of scented oil to it.

A simple passive diffuser is a shallow oil dish that you make from self-hardening clay. Alternatively, you can make a reed model by recycling a wee vase: Pour some essential oil into the vessel and then vertically insert hollow dried reeds or the frayed ends of inexpensive wooden skewers or chopsticks.[90] The oil will defy gravity and wick upward. Relish the subtle scent these passive diffusers release for weeks and months.

Books abound listing the aromatic and magical benefits of essential oils, and free lists proliferate on the Internet as well. All natural kinds of essential oils derive from combustible plants and woods. Mind your magical correspondences when choosing what to use.

Change the scent profile to mirror the smell in the air with the changing of the seasons. Use one to improve your mood, another to set the tone for a Witch ritual, and yet another to provoke sex or induce sleep.

Adding herbs or spices to diffuser oil isn't recommended, because they can mat, mold, and encourage the oil to go rancid. If you would gild the lily, add stone chips, seashells, and similar inorganic items instead.

---

90 Each time you change the oil, supply fresh reeds, skewers, or chopsticks.

LAMP SPELLS

As intimated above, *The Goodly Spellbook* explains that the Greeks reserved red lamps to cultivate and revere their Ancestors and Lares (household Gods—plural in Italian, *Lasii*). Therefore, their written lamp spells often specifically *prohibited* using a red lamp to perform any other kind of spellwork.

The Ones Who Came Before (a Witch phrase meaning ancient Pagans) cleansed their spellwork lamps before use by washing them with natron salt water. Witches use consecrated salt water to this day. To further consecrate salt water, which already contains the two sacred Elements of salt and water, pass the vessel it's in through incense smoke and then candle flame.

To minimize their burn risk, the ancients routinely set their magic lamps atop a "new brick."[91] Ancient Pagans might imprecate for favor with their mouths pressed directly upon the lamp's surface and, akin to the Italian tradition of threatening a deity to grant a plea, feign withholding fuel or desecrating the vessel if they felt particularly exercised about a matter:

"If thou wilt not do it, I will not give thee oil. . . . I will not give thee fat. O lamp; verily I will give thee the body of the female cow[92] and put blood of the male bull into thee. . . ."

—Col. VI. Demotic text

Pagans in antiquity oft relied on an innocent boy[93] to act as an entranced intercessor and interface with the God/desses on their behalf. Families were large and extended back then, and boys abounded throughout the household.

Typically, the male master of the home would ask a boy to aid his magic and have him sit atop a brick opposite the brick on which the magic lamp resided. The man of the house would then ask the lamp questions and rely on the boy to relate divine answers by the boy's scrying and interpreting the lamp flame's vigor or lethargy. Ceremonial magicians continued the boy-seer practice throughout the Renaissance and for centuries beyond.

Young, psychically-inclined or magically-gifted maiden girls can be equally, if not superior, in serving as oracles in this traditional query endeavor.

---

91 The source, Col. XXV *The Demotic Magical Papyrus of London and Leiden*, specifies this as one "brought from the mould makes and clean, on which no man has mounted"—probably, trod on or having been previously used to build.
92 Beef flesh and blood meant to pollute or desecrate the lamp if it did not aid the querent.
93 A virgin "who has not yet gone with a woman." Source, Col. XXV *The Demotic Magical Papyrus of London and Leiden*.

The following is a succession of fascinating ancient lamp spells that will enable you to work all manner of fire magic. The spelling is as written in antiquity and published eons later.

ANCIENT MORNING SUCCESS SPELLS

You can work a spell to attract success, but the following *PGM* oil lamp spell and alternative will ensure it, particularly when you're nervous because circumstances seem crucial, fraught, or worrisome.

The invocation which you pronounce before Phre[94] in the morning . . . in order that that which thou doest may succeed:

"O GREAT GOD, TABAO, BASOUKHAM, AMO, AKHAKHARKHAN-KRABOUN-ZANOUNI-EDIKOMTO, KETHOU-BASA-THOURI-THMILA-ALO." Seven times.

Another method of it again. You rise in the morning from your bed early in the day on which you will do it, or any day, in order that every thing which you will do shall prosper in your hand, you being pure from every abomination. You pronounce this invocation before Phre three times or seven times:

"LO, TABAO, SOKHOM-MOA, OKH-OKH-KHAN-BOUZANAU, AN-IESI, EKOMPHTHO, KETHO, SETHOURI, THMILA, ALOUAPOKHRI, LET EVERYTHING THAT I SHALL APPLY MY HAND TO HERE TO-DAY, LEI IT HAPPEN."

LAMPLIGHT LYCHNOMANCY

As a fire speaks volumes by its sound and fury, so a powerful being can inhabit a lamp and communicate through it. Perform lamp divination (also called lampadomancy) to conjure the spirit of the fire to reveal secrets, wisdom, or future events.

After sunset on a Monday when the moon is new or waning, apply an enabling eye paint such as soot, kohl, black eyeliner, Gothic eye shadow, or reconstituted

94 ". . . the glorious boy-God whom they call Gartaby"; originally the Egyptian Sun God Re, later the Sun God Horus, son of Isis and Osiris. This means you should perform the spell adoors while facing the sunrise. Source: *The Demotic Magical Papyrus*.

powdered date fruit pit and then work this spell from Verso Col. XXVI:[95]

If you wish to make the gods of the vessel speak with you, when the gods come in, you say this name to them nine times:

"LAHO, IPHE, EOE, KINTATHOUR, NEPHAR, APHOE."

Then he makes command to you as to that which you shall ask him about.

If delay occur, so that answer is not given you, you recite this other name to them.[96] nine times until they inquire for you truthfully:

"GOGETHIX, MANTOU, NOBOE, KHOKHIR, HRODOR, DONDROMA, LEPHOKER, KEPHAERSORE."

SLEEP SPELLS

TO REQUEST A DREAM ORACLE

The following oil lamp spell invokes the Egyptian lioness Goddess Sekmet and God Set to provide insight during dream.[97]

Take a Strip of Clean Linen and write on it the following Name. Roll it up to make a Wick, pour Pure Olive Oil over it, and light it.[98] The Formula to be written is this:

HARMIOUTH LAILAM CHO'OUCH ARSENOPHRE' PHRE'U PHTHA HARCHENTECHTHA.

In the Evening then, when you are about to go to Sleep, being Pure in every respect, do this: Go to the Lamp, say 7 times the following Formula, extinguish the Light, and go to Sleep.

The Formula to be spoken is as follows:

"SACHMOUNE [I.E., SAKHMET] PAE'MALIGOTE'RE'E'NCH, THE ONE WHO SHAKES, WHO THUNDERS, WHO HAS SWALLOWED THE SERPENT, SURROUNDS THE MOON, AND HOUR BY HOUR RAISES

---

95 Ibid.
96 The God inquires about the question posed to Him and truthfully reveals an answer to the spellcaster.
97 From *PGM* VII.359-69.
98 Burn it in a clay olive oil lamp or something similar.

THE DISK OF THE SUN, CHTHETHO'NI IS YOUR NAME. I ASK YOU,
LORDS OF THE GODS, SE'TH CHRE'PS: REVEAL TO ME CONCERNING
THE THINGS I WISH."

TO APPEAR IN ANOTHER'S DREAM

One way to win the love of your dreams is to appear in his or her dreams. You can
also use this oil lamp spell from *PGM VII.407—10* to cut through a person's defenses
and extol your virtues to your love interest while they are vulnerable during dream—
the possibilities are myriad and intriguing. Pronounce the Words *"Kee'ahmo p'see
Urpee-boat."*

If you wish to appear to Someone at Night in Dreams, say to the Lamp that is in
daily use,[99] say frequently:

"CHEIAMO'PSEI ERPEBO'TH, LET HER, NN,[100] WHOM NN BORE,[101]
SEE ME IN HER DREAMS, IMMEDIATELY, IMMEDIATELY; QUICKLY,
QUICKLY!" [and add the usual, whatever you wish].

---

99 In antiquity, a lamp burned in honor of the Lares, or spirits of the home occupants' ancestors, typically tended and spelled
to by a maiden of the household.
100 In ancient grimoires "NN" signifies "insert appropriate name," in this case your love target. If your target is male, change
the gender of the pronouns.
101 NN's biological mother.

CANDLE MAGIC: WITCHY USES OF CANDLES

"I think candlelight is the most beautiful light there is and there's something very spiritual about it."

—Nicole Kidman, Oscar®-winning actress

G low. Snatching sight of the wild white of a participant's eye in a candlelit ritual room. Candles give off shade, shadow light, so feel free to think outside the box by using floating candles or thrift store champagne glasses filled with oil, with a floating wick atop them.

Keep the lighting muted, lively, diverse, and actively manipulate light and shadow so that you and rite participants look awesome and feel duly Witchy.

KINDS OF WITCH CANDLES

Traditional Witch candles were often made of dried, twined bullrushes, cattails, or melted beeswax mixed with soot or tallow—rendered beef or mutton fat processed from suet. Tallow doesn't require refrigeration to prevent it from going rancid as long as you store it well and minimize oxidation (exposure to air). Wicks were twisted or woven from treated papyrus, livestock hair, rags—basically anything that could catch alight with minimal risk of burning the holder.

Another kind of olde Witch taper was made of one long, fresh fuzzy mullein leaf[102] rolled like a cigar and then drenched with cooled bacon drippings.

These days, candles come in a dazzling array of wax types colors, shapes, sizes, and styles. They have diverse wax bases, scents, and textural inclusions such as stones, jewelry, and herbs. You can make your own beeswax and coconut, soy, or palm oil votives, or shop online for, say, a black skull candle or waxen, wicked human figures.

---

102 Common herb name, lamb's ear because it is as soft as and resembles one.

Paraffin is clear or whitish and can come in bars, flakes, or beads. It's an inexpensive popular wax but is petroleum/hydrocarbon-based (of which some Pagans revile). Paraffin melts easily and shows inclusions well.

Beeswax is natural, too, but has skyrocketed in price as a consequence of bee colony collapse believed caused by humans' ubiquitous application of pesticides that negatively impact the bees' immunity, pollution, techno or military vibrations that make them loose their way to the hive, as well as by invasive predator species and new disease states. Beeswax melts slowly and its natural opaque dull orange color can obscure inclusions, which can be a virtue if you want them to be a surprise revealed as the candle burns down and melts away. Its natural honey-colored hue can be difficult to affect or overcome by adding a color dye.

Soy and palm oil–based candles are currently in vogue. Soy has a consistency in between that of paraffin and beeswax, and similarly to the latter, it emits a natural scent of its own.

Some candles are intricately carved or molded, with pictures or wedding invitations viewable beneath a translucent wax window on the candles' surface. Other candles are seven-knobbed to allow you to burn one per day to work one candle magic spell over a weekday period.

Still other kinds come in split color combinations such as half red and half black: These are called "reversing," "cursing," or "hex candles." They start angry (red) and then settle into a binding black designed to protect the spellcaster burner from enduring further attack or harm from a perceived threat or a menacing person. However, a case could be made that you could burn the black half *first* to acknowledge a bad situation, and then burn the red half to induce love and push back against the poisonous problem. It is up to you, really—just be clear on your intention and burn the colors that reflect your issue and desired spell outcome.

Even as I wrote this, the Yankee Candle Company™ had begun a media push to encourage people to go online and personalize a candle by color and fragrance and to upload any picture they wanted with which to decorate it. My magical mind boggles at the potential to affect political elections, incline a pic of a judge in a court context, attract love, bind a threat, heal someone, nurture the planet, or secure justice denied, etc.

When it comes to candles, size doesn't matter but color and scent count. You can use one as small as a weensy birthday candle to work wicked magic, and I've done so when pressed, on the floor of a hotel bathroom of all sacrilegious places.

Although most magic is planned, you can work magic at any time during an emergency situation.

Male and female human figure candles are popular, but I consider them a magical cheat because it's far better to make a poppet of a person by hand from melted wax than to buy a generic model that may bear minimal resemblance to your troubling or troubled target. These are initially worked as a simulacrum of the person in absentia, and later burned as the spell's capper finale. However, one appropriate use of a manufactured figure candle would be to aid or heal someone from afar when you've never met them in person.

Some candles come with a lid that's helpful to smother the flame. When the wax has burned down, these tins or glass jars can be washed and repurposed as a portable ashtray; for storing dried herbs, tea, or resin incense; as a gem repository or micro-sized spell kit container; to keep rolled hemp string in; as a stash jar for blind nettle (the Witch word for *Cannabis sativa*), and so forth.

Humanity will perpetually continue to experiment with producing candles from diverse oils and waxes such as coconut oil, waxy berries, and hemp oil. Not only do they all possess unique merits and magically correspond with the seasons, planets, and other universal powers, there's something in our souls that stirs, thrills, and delights in the dance of firelight and summer lightning bugs, and that detests being suppressed by blinding-bright business office florescent lighting.

MAGICAL CANDLE COLOR CORRESPONDENCES

You don't have to make your own candles. Just buy wisely to further your mystical aims.

On Coven Oldenwilde's main Eastern direction altar we use the Gardnerian default setup: A red (or white) candle that represents the Goddess on the left as you're facing the altar, a similar candle representing the God on the right as you're facing the altar, and between the two, a third candle representing either the Maiden aspect of the Goddess or Drychton (pronounced *Drichk*-ton or *Dry*-ton), a Gardnerian Witch name for the neuter All-spirit.

Of course other, smaller candles can be added hither and thither to any altar if space allows, and our other three Quarter directional altars (South, West, and North) sport all manner of color-corresponding candles everywhere. The candles drip of their own accord and often show by their responsiveness or lethargy that they want to be placed here versus there, or react to our spellwork in producing image omens by how they form their drips like liquid paint strokes or shapes.

You need not be as ritualistic to work wicked wax magic: Burn a candle as the mood strikes, or one, two, or more for a highly motivated spell purpose. Have many or as few as desired or as life circumstances enable or limit.

We detailed color correspondences in *The Goodly Spellbook*. Here is a quick cheat sheet to refer to in choosing a candle color to correspond magically to your spell intention.

It is based on the day of the week (and, by extension, the hours during each night and day) that the seven major planets rule[103] to enable you to work specific kinds of magic and have the heavenly bodies amplify it with their sway thusly:

* SUNDAY—Sun God solar orange or twilight pink

* MONDAY—Gray, silver, or white as the Moon Goddess

* TUESDAY—Red as the God Mars in His warrior aspect

* WEDNESDAY—Yellow (sacred to the East direction and communication or when you want your opinion or rationale to win an argument)

* THURSDAY—Blue (sacred to Thor and Neptune) or purple (sacred to the abundance God Jupiter and God/desses of boon and beneficence)

* FRIDAY—Green (for the friendly fertility Goddess Freya)

* SATURDAY—Black (sacred to taciturn Saturn, the planet-God of boundaries)

Or you can choose your candle color to evoke optimal aid from the God/desses depending on your particular desire, issue, need, or rite.

* BEIGE—blandness, boredom, conformity, grain, matron.

* BLACK—ancestors, antiquity, boundaries, cloaking, craft clergy, croning ritual, cursing, death, depth, evil, fear, hexing, invisibility, magical mastery, North, relationship breakup, repression, Rite for the Departed Soul, sleep, tenacity, third-degree Elevation ritual.

---

103 Explained and illustrated in the section "Planetary Days and Hours," *The Goodly Spellbook*, Lady Passion and *Diuvei, Sterling Publishing, 2005, 2014.

* BLUE—audacity, bliss, boy, depression, fish, ocean, rain, river, sadness, sea, trust, water, weeping, West.

* BROWN—bread, home, humility, soil.

* CLEAR—honesty, invisibility, truth.

* GOLD—avarice, business, coin, day, greed, health, heat, men, occupation, ownership, power, treasure, value, wealth.

* GRAY—concern, confusion, doubt, ghost haunting, indecision, nebulous angst, past life regression, rock, worry.

* GREEN—body, conception, crops, Earth, environment, envy, fertility, fields, food, gangrene, grass, Green Manning ritual, healing, herbs, infection, jealousy, land, luck, North, plants, shelter, territory, treasure, trees.

* ORANGE—agitation, energy, South, vibrancy.

* PINK—flirtation, girl, idealistic love, maidens, naiveté, South, youth.

* PURPLE—abundance, aspiration, dream, New Age spirituality, spirit, transcendence.

* RED—aggression, anger, attack, attraction, bloodshed, courage, danger, fever, fire, force, hate, ire, love/lust, persecution, protest, rage, sacrifice, second-degree Elevation ritual, seduction, sensuality, sex, South, temptation, violence, volcanoes, war.

* SILVER—cool, divination, foresight, intuition, magic, a teen girl's Moon-time rite of passage, night, occult, secrets, women.

* TURQUOISE—friendship, indigenous cultures.

* WHITE—A newborn's Wiccaning rite of passage, Air, communication, death in some cultures, East, first-degree Witch initiation ritual, innocence, inspiration, intellect, lactation, learning, light, memory, milk, mind, nuptials, opinion, purity, reincarnation, sleet, speech, snow, soul, stars, thought, virginity, wind, winter, wisdom.

* YELLOW—cowardice, East, hope, recovery.

Ponder and experiment with using more magical color correspondences in combination, such as puce (gray-green), rust (red-brown), and slate (silvery black).

CANDLE-MAKING RECIPES

"I love having candles . . . I could just pass out seeing the flame flicker with the lights off."

—Kellan Lutz, actor

Many, many books have been written illustrating simple, complicated, and creative ways to make, decorate with, and use candles in spiritual and sensual contexts.

Certainly you can make Yule gift candles by melting paraffin, pouring it into a washed plasticized paper frozen juice concentrate container, and inserting a wick, as many elementary school kids are taught to do. Or you can embellish store-bought candles or seriously invest and buy metal molds and then release fixative sprays, chemical preservatives, carving tools, and so on.

Making candles can become your magical specialty, but since fire magic is only one of mine, I see no reason to rephrase other authors to repeat their detail, as candle making is worthy of an entire book of its own. I encourage you to search online, peruse library books, or buy a few books on the subject such as *Candlemaking The Natural Way: 31 Projects Made With Soy, Palm & Beeswax*, by Rebecca Ittner (Lark Crafts/Sterling Publishing, 2011). These tomes are replete with inspiring illustrations, the history of candles' impact on humanity, lists of needed ingredients, glossaries of terms, expert tips, and creative, cost-effective shortcuts.

However, having made candles for some time and coming at them from a specifically magical focus, I can impart wisdom and spells that these arts-and-crafts books don't include.

WITCH CANDLE TIPS

"Lighting candles should never be done indifferently or with lack of intention."

—W. G. Gray, English ceremonial magician, 1913–1992

MAGICAL RITUAL METHODS

A quick and easy way to hand make dozens of ritual candles in a flash is to buy a package of pre-waxed wicks and flat sheets of honeycomb cell–stamped beeswax online or from an arts-and-crafts store and horizontally roll-wrap the wick into the sheet as you would if you were wielding a rolling pin to make pizza dough.

The sheets allow you to readily customize the height and width of your candle with easy scissor cutting, or by adding extra sheets onto previously rolled sheets.

If the candle ends "dome outward" from your rolling and the result isn't straight enough to stand upright in a candleholder, hold it upright atop a hot metal pot and melt a tad off each until it's flat.

Embellish the candles if you wish by tying a weensy explanatory scroll, earring, or pendant around them using raffia, or by sticking a Witchy hatpin in their side, among other methods.

The recipe for melting wax to make a candle or a waxen poppet of a person is in *The Goodly Spellbook*, but basically calls for a rudimentary double-boiler setup (a small pot inside a large pot half filled with water atop a heat source such as a stove burner). Put solid, hard wax in the large pot over water inside the smaller pot until it melts, and then remove the wick with tongs or a chopstick.

You can snip the plastic ends off a shoelace to make emergency candle wicking, buy it in many lengths and widths on a spool,[104] buy lantern wicks that are thicker and can burn brighter, or buy them by the bagful with small round metal settings to stabilize the wick on the bottom of the candle included. Some even come pre-waxed.

If you're Witchy curious and daring, you can easily learn how to drop-spindle spin and braid your own wicks from combed wool. Books and sites online provide easy instructions for using a stick inserted into a roundel and using gravity to spin a triangle of handheld brushed wool into thread, how to twist two threads woven in opposite directions to add strength, and how to hang dry and even dye them if desired.

Many drop spindles are pocket portable and can be acquired in ceramic, wood, and even metal form. They can be new or antique, and many consider them collectibles.

Combed wool for making wicks is available from many countries worldwide and comes in a huge variety of tensile strengths, colors, ombre-dyed styles, and thicknesses and delicacies. I have pounds of raw un-dyed wool and everything in between down to breathy silver strands that seem spun by fairies.

You can also take single-strand hemp string and braid it by looping a length around your toe, or buy several strands pre-braided together, cut it in a length to suit, and dip it in melted wax to make a strong, long-burning wick.

---

104 The #2 or #3 sizes work well for making most types of candles.

However, if your wick isn't recycled from the melted wax of a previous candle or if you bought it un-waxed, always dip it in melted wax and dry it horizontally flat atop wax paper to enable it to stand upright, drip less, and burn more steadily and long.

Always allow for a bit of extra length on both ends that you *don't* dip in wax, or strip some wax off after the waxed wick dries. This allows you to more easily trim the wick atop and at the candle base to suit your candle length. You can take a day to do naught but wax wicks and then melt and pour candles the next day.

To center the wick in your candle, weight the bottom of it down in the center of your container or mold by tying one of the wick's ends onto a dime or pull it though an inexpensive lightweight aluminum wick stabilizer. Tie the other end of the wick onto a pencil, skewer, or chopstick and center-balance it horizontally across the container or mold's top and then pour in the melted wax.

When your candle is fully dry, use scissors to snip the top of the wick off about 1/8 inch (3mm) above the candle's top and remove it from the mold or leave it as is if you made a non-removable candle in a pretty glass jar or champagne flute.

CREATIVE AND EMERGENCY CANDLE RECIPES

Witches love natural molds such as vegetables, fruit, and paper and loathe being caught unprepared during a power outage or not having the right colored candle to work immediate magic.

We want big pillars and mini-candles, liquid oil and solid wax options, and savvy shortcuts and easy instructions that produce original art.

The following candle-making recipes aren't of the typical "melt crayons in an orange juice container" type: They feature cutting-edge creativity and Craft ingenuity.

CINNAMON PUMPKIN MINI-CANDLE

Horizontally slice a mini-pumpkin in half. Use a spoon to remove the vegetable matter inside both halves. Melt beeswax in a double-boiler setup on a stovetop burner.

Wax two wicks and air-dry them atop wax paper. Stir ground cinnamon into the liquid, using a chopstick. Set each wick inside a pumpkin half, using the balanced pencil method.

Pour wax into each half. Briefly quick dry in the freezer if desired. This yields two candles.

CAFÉ CANDLE

Scent your home like French vanilla or chocolate coffee. Recycle a vintage coffee cup and saucer or demitasse set that you rarely use to serve as a mold. Glue the bottom of the cup to the upturned center of the saucer.

Tie one end of a wick onto a pencil. Melt two or three beige taper candles in a double-boiler setup atop a stovetop burner. Fish out the wicks and quickly dry flat and straight atop wax paper in the freezer.

Next, pick a wick and hold it straight in the center of the cup with one hand while you gently pour the liquid wax into the cup. When it has set enough to hold the wick upright, add whole coffee beans and vanilla beans. Stir with a chopstick to distribute both a bit away from the wick to reduce the chance of their catching alight. Trim the wick about ¼ inch (6mm) above the dried candle and light.

Prevent beans catching alight by using a mortar and pestle or an electric coffee grinder to pulverize them in separate batches. Or you can produce a mocha scent by substituting pinches of cocoa powder for vanilla beans.

NUTSHELL FAIRY CANDLE

If you're not allergic to them, buy a bag of whole walnuts. Use a nutcracker to open several of them in perfect halves. If you lack a nutcracker, try sandwiching one nut at a time between bubble wrap and whacking it with a hammer or rubber mallet. Dig out and eat the nut meat.

Next, melt used candle stubs in a double boiler setup. Fish out the wicks and dry them horizontally atop wax paper on a flat surface. Carefully drizzle the liquid wax into the empty shell halves. Then insert a tiny wick into the center of the wax in each half. Air-dry the wax until it congeals solid.

Place a few of the wee lights adoors on your patio, porch, or terrace as an offering to the Seely Court of "happy, lucky, blessed" fairies, or indoors to decorate your home or ritual space.

ORANGE FRUIT CANDLE

Use a small, sharp paring knife to slice an orange in half horizontally through the outer peel. Part the halves and then slide your fingers or fingernails beneath the rind and gently remove the fruit without tearing the peel shells. Find the stem—a white fleshy projection inside the peel—in the center of the bottom half of the orange. The longer this natural "wick" is, the longer the candle will burn.

Pour three or so tablespoons of olive oil onto this wick and let it absorb for three minutes or more. Light by using long fireplace matches or a long-barreled lighter.

ORANGE FRUIT CANDLE ALTERNATIVE

Decorate a semi-protective lid for your orange candle. Flip inside-out the top half of a de-pulped orange. Use a permanent marker to draw a stencil-type design atop the white pith. Designs can include crescent moons or stars with open centers, or similar magical symbols.

Use a sharp knife to cut out your design from the rind. Flip the half bright side out again and top the burning orange candle with it so that the light emanates through your magical design symbols.

ICED MILK CANDLE

Rinse clean and then dry an empty milk carton. Open the carton top fully. Melt some previously burned candles of the same color. Remove their wicks from the liquid and discard them.

Now cut a new wick to the length desired. Tie one end of it to a pencil and let the other end dangle straight down to the bottom of the mold. Balance the pencil atop the mold.

Next, fill the carton with enough whole frozen ice cubes to cover with wax. Pour wax into the mold as low or high as desired, such as 3 inches (7.62cm) above the bottom for more squat candles, or fully up to near the brim. Cool the candle at room temperature for two hours or so and then pour the melted ice water into the trash.

Next, tear off the paper mold and trim the wick as needed. This recipe produces lovely holey-textured candles.

Tip: Pale yellow-colored wax resembles a block of Swiss cheese.

EMERGENCY MINI-CANDLES

When you need to cast an urgent spell but realize that you're out of the right colored candle to magically correspond to your intent, find a crayon in that color, remove its paper wrapper, and light it: One will burn for about half an hour.

EMERGENCY OLIVE OIL CANDLES

Stock a few clear glass, wide-bottom pint jars, a spool of #2 or lantern wicking, and a spool of metal craft wire. If a power outage occurs or if you crave romantic lighting or want a clear candle, grab your jars. Then do the following:

Cut the wick to the desired length. Twist one end of the wire around one end of the wick so that it stands upright in the center of the jar with about ¼ inch (6mm) projecting above the wire. Twist the other end of the wire so that it rests around the threads on one side of the jar and further stabilizes the wick in place.

Now pour olive oil into the jar. Add a few drops of an essential oil to scent the oil if you wish. Let the wick absorb the oil for several minutes before lighting. Make several at a time if you want candles in multiple rooms.

SCENTED CANDLES

> "I'm a great lighter and lover of candles, particularly fragranced ones, as I'm kind of addicted to scent."
>
> —Deirdre O'Kane, Irish actress

Scent allows you to personalize magical candles and can be used in lieu of burning incense, but your choice of scent should always magically correspond with, and therefore, support, your spell intention. Consider the planetary correspondences of scents provided in *The Goodly Spellbook*, as well as the color correspondences described above.

For instance, lavender sprigs are purple and hence should be goodly for conjuring beneficence from the abundance planet Jupiter, which is associated with the color purple. Similarly, rose petals are soft, so it stands to reason that their scent should be goodly for attracting love or softening the wrath of someone who's angry with you.

In the same vein, because its scent is sharp, pine would be inappropriate to use if you were casting a curse: Clean-smelling candles for sickrooms, healing, or well-meaning should be scented with a "high note" such as pine, eucalyptus, lotus, or clary sage, whereas for cursing you'd want to burn something noxiously scented such as mugwort or asafetida.

If you gift a scented candle, consider the recipient's personality and proclivities and aversions. For instance, if you know your Covenmates' different natal Sun signs, you can make a candle for each as a Yule gift that reflects each one's particular affinities and planetary influences, such as a Watery sea salt–scented Pisces candle, a *caliente* spice-scented Leo candle, an Airy eucalyptus-scented Libra candle, or a peat moss-scented candle for an Earthy Virgo.

And if you know the nature of your Covenmates exceedingly well, you could even go in an opposite direction and gift them with a candle that would *counter* their detriments, such as grounding an Airy indecisive Gemini with an Earthy brown-black candle, uplifting a depressive Capricorn with an Airy yellow candle, or pulling an Earth sign out of his or her comfy rut with an energizing orange candle.

A few drops are all it takes to scent a candle, but until you get your preferred recipe proportions down, it can be challenging to know before the wax fully cools how the candle will actually smell when burned.

Fear not making mistakes, for it's rather normal when you work with a fluid medium with which you're unfamiliar. Instead, take heart that you can always scrap a lot and re-melt failure bits into new, unique candles or break up the wax, tie loosely-woven scrap fabric around them, and use them in a drawer as sachets. Wax is as perpetual a forgiving medium as it is initially challenging to master.

HERB, GEM, AND CHARM INCLUSION

If you make candles by hand, feel free to add shells, dried herbs, gem chips, or silver charms to the hot wax when it begins semi-air-drying; otherwise, they are apt to sink to the bottom of your mold or container when you'd probably prefer that they be more equally distributed throughout the candle wax.

Or you can sprinkle inclusions on a piece of wax paper, quickly dip the candle in melted wax, and then roll it onto the inclusions so that they decorate its outside (if it's a taper, it's best to do this above the top of a candleholder).

BIGRAVING CANDLES

Imbue molded pillar, taper, or votive candles with extra power and obscure your spell purpose from prying eyes by bigraving[105] appropriate occult symbols and/or spell words in a magical script along their shafts or under their bases. The effect is artistic, and it cloaks Witches' concern about eliciting needless disapproval from family, friends, and nosey neighbors.

---

105 The Witch word for engraving.

This can be as simple as carving an all-purpose protective pentagram to burn for any occasion, or as intricate as a spell sentence in the Theban script fit to burn for a specific reason.

The Goodly Spellbook illustrates the meaning and uses of many magical symbols and traditional Witch alphabets. The easiest mystical script to use to inscribe on typically rounded candle surfaces are Ogham, which features horizontal and diagonal slash marks on a vertical line base, and Runic, which is similar in that it uses only straight lines, but is more elaborate because each letter is composed of varying *angles* of straight marks. Passing the River and Theban magical alphabets are more intricate yet, and Egyptian hieroglyphs are the most challenging to master.

All provoke different emotions: Ogham evokes collective memories of Paleolithic cave paintings, Runic strikes the heart like a mighty sword, Passing the River feels mysteriously medieval, and Theban is like watching French ballerinas dance.

If you carve tapers top to bottom with Egyptian hieroglyphs, always surround your vertical string of symbols with a cartouche—a rope/lasso-like encirclement in the shape of a pastry éclair, and the origin of the protective circle (or even more traditional, *double* circles that surround Witches' religious symbol, the upright pentagram). This cartouche protects, contains, and amplifies the magical power of your candle's encryption.

There are many "dead" languages,[106] arcane languages, poorly known languages, and languages and symbols from other countries that most folk who know you do not know and wouldn't have a clue how to research, decipher, and therefore interfere with your Work. Use any of these alphabets, letters, or glyphs to obscure your magical intention from prying eyes: If they even notice it at all, most folk will simply assume it's decorative.

The Goodly Spellbook also illustrates geomancy—the Art Magical of divining by making random dots—16 sets of which have great meaning. You can create a sentence string using geomancy dots or Morse code dots and dashes as well.

A similar option is to use dots to convey Braille letters. Based on the configuration of six cells of dots that resemble domino dots, Braille is easy to learn and inscribe, and free alphabetical translations of it in many languages and in mathematical numbers, musical notations, and scientific terms exist online and in library books. If you feel insecure about carving slashes, much less flourishes, straight pin pricks on a candle's outer surface will suffice.

---

106 Not yet deciphered, politically suppressed, or fallen from favor—in short, no longer spoken or widely used.

Regardless of your choice, the concentration that you put into the effort to get it right without slipping and nicking the delicate wax in unwanted ways reminds you to give equal focus not only to magical candles, but by extension, to your ritual spellwork.

If you haven't memorized it, print out or draw your selected symbol or magical script ahead of time and refer to it as needed while bigraving your candle. Sit comfortably in your kitchen or cross-legged on your ritual room floor; warm the tip of your boline, burin, or similar sharp object in candle flame; and set to work. As always, approach magic with boldness, particularly when wielding a sharp object.

Many Witches find it helpful to chant or sing while they bigrave candles, in order to steady the hand and set up a calm, competent rhythm for carving the strokes.

Bigraving is not a requisite for magical candle work, but you should at least try to become proficient in it. Its merit is that it's yet another layer of magic, and Witches' renowned power lies in layering magic until the scales of justice tip in our favor.

Practice makes perfect, but even crude scribbling can lend an air of primal power, so forgive yourself for your minor imperfections until the skill feels familiar: After all, they don't teach Witch tricks in school.

"DRESSING" CANDLES WITH OILS

Some Witches prefer to make or buy unscented candles, and this is fine because it's traditional to magically "dress" them with a scented or essential oil *after* bigraving them; doing things in this order forfends avoidable injury caused by oily slipperiness while carving wax with a sharp object.

"Scented" oils are typically synthetic, are a blend of different oils, or are thinned with a base such as mineral oil in order to stretch their volume and increase the seller's profits. An example of a synthetic oil is anything labeled "Egyptian Moon Goddess" or the like. Synthetic oils are cost-effective compared with essential oils.

Essential oils are "pure"—unblended and with minimal or no thinning. An example of an essential oil is Rose Absolute distilled from the flower's petals. Some essential oils derive from endangered species, such as musk from Civit cats, or ambergris from the bile duct of sperm whales.[107] Because essentials oils are traditional and can be expensive, they are treasured and therefore, make precious sacrifice offerings

---

107 Ambergris forms over many years' time, and can be gleaned from atop sea waves or even removed from the stomach of a deceased sperm whale.

to the Gods. Essential oils are concentrated and enable you to use less of the liquid to produce both subtle and intense effects.

Add yet another layer of power to your candle work by "dressing" (anointing) them by topically applying to their outside surface a scented or essential oil. To magically dress a candle, smooth on the oil using your left fingers, beginning from its middle and spiraling down toward its base, and then resuming in the middle and spiraling upward to its top.

I don't recommend anointing candles' bases, as this will interfere with your ability to set the candle securely upright in a candleholder by dripping a few drops of liquid wax on the holder's inner base. Skip the wick as well, as that would impede it from catching alight.

In summary: If your candle is unscented, you *can* bigrave it, but if you do, only anoint it *thereafter*. If you skip the bigraving step, simply anoint the candle before use.

MAKING CANDLEHOLDERS

Candles aren't the *only* fire components that can be dressed in scented oil. You can also anoint candleholders with desirable scents, particularly if you prefer to make or purchase unscented candles.

Candlesticks and candleholders come in a dazzling array of shapes, sizes, colors, compositions, and varieties. Always check the radius and depth of the base reservoir of a candlestick, for some are small and shallow and therefore require small, difficult to find candles to fit them, whereas others have an "endless" reservoir that can extend to the bottom, making it difficult to thoroughly remove drip-hardened wax. Also, always note candleholders with intricate filigree patterns, as they can also be difficult to keep dusted pristine.

Silver or copper candleholders are traditional but require routine polishing to forfend tarnish, yet most Witches continue to appreciate the goodly patina that comes from some handling and use over time.

Pewter and states-metal are less expensive modern alternatives. Pewter varieties are heavy enough to double as a protective weapon if needed. Neither requires frequent polishing to maintain its luster, which is only slightly less than that of silver. Inexpensive brass candleholders abound, and are best set in the South direction. Copper also goes in the fiery South circle direction, but is more expensive and patinas green over time.

Wooden candleholders are prone to split in twain from the effect of candle heat, or to catch alight outright as well as to dry out from washing, and can chip when you take a boline to them to remove dried wax remnants from them after ritual.

THE TALLOW CANDLE.

Carved stone candleholders must be treated with care because they are innately delicate and are vulnerable to cracking from candle-flame heat and to shattering if accidentally dropped on the floor. Examples include polished agate, bored amethyst or crystal clusters, and volcanic ash that is pulverized, mixed with liquid, and turned to stone in an mold, and then decoratively carved by indigenous folk.

Crystal clusters are best only dusted, as it's exceedingly difficult to scrape dried wax from cold stone, and the rust, impurity, and additive content in common tap water can discolor their reflection by seeping into micro-cracks in the stone and encourage it to occlude or split asunder. Because of this, I tend to only use battery-operated tea lights in this type of candleholder.

Glass and ceramic holders are oft the most cost effective for Pagans on a budget, but are fragile. Both can shatter from the candle and explode into shards that are difficult to see and sweep up. More than most kinds of candleholders, glass tends to show flame soot, so if it presents, keep the holder sparkly by washing this off after each use.

Other organic candleholder kinds include: Carved chunks of Himalayan rock salt holders and holders that Asian Indians make from Ganges river mud on their potter's wheels: the former will melt in sunlight or summer heat, so try to park such a holder in a darkish cool corner.

Considering these challenges, it's understandable that from abracadabra to candelabra, Witches continue to favor silver or copper candleholders. Yet in typical Pagan paradox fashion, we *also* believe in the principle of "the more, the merrier" because we see life in all its beautiful complexity, its natural diversity and, therefore, we feel strongly that we must remain lively on our feet in order to thrive. It's this last belief that encourages us to make candleholders out of a *variety* of things that others wouldn't—antique champagne glasses from a thrift store, homemade Play-doh®, seashells, a large animal's backbone—all manner of things.

There's *power* in appreciating diversity, in employing multiple magical means, alternatives, approaches, ingredients, and inclusions. More food is better than less, and, by extension, we feel that the more candles we have, the more options we possess when things go awry, we feel this way versus that, or we need or want something specific that only one particular candle or holder could best manifest.

I have all these types of candleholders and more, and use them to affect specific magic depending on their unique virtues that are based on their composition.

One of my favorites is recycling tempered glass baby-food jars or small tumblers from thrift stores or garage sales and setting wax tea lights in their bases. I love the ghostly Witchy figures and shapes that the melted wax forms inside the glass when the flame is extinguished. When the jar is tilted a bit aggressively, the liquid wax swirls and creates all manner of phantasmic shapes that dry and naturally decorate the exterior of the glass from the inside. I have these by the hundred, and they make goodly picnic table altar lighting for large public rites and gatherings.

A similar effect using recycled baby-food jars is achieved by twisting craft wire around and upward between their outer jar-top threads and then insetting votive candles inside and hanging the lamps. This decor is an inexpensive, ecological, and inspiring touch when suspended from trees or eaves.

I put tea light candles in large seashells and set wider wax tea lights in the vertebral holes of mammal backbones and hip bones. The latter look wicked cool in front of my Covenstead's ritual room North Quarter altar.

I have also cut leather to house a large glass dome inset with tea lights and hung it from the ceiling of the circling space. These, along with various metallic silver and iron dimensional pentagrams with glass panels, adorn the Covenstead throughout and provide a myriad of lighting options.

I never simply burn a candle set inside my cauldron, however, because wax spatters and drips and is extremely difficult to scrape off the iron. When I *do* burn candles in my cauldron, they are either ones that float on water, or pillars inset in a container that prevents spattering and dripping, such as a clear glass vase or a "cup up" glass urn; the candles are then set in sand or dirt and typically are surrounded by river stones, seashells, or some similar natural decoration.

Another favorite candle centerpiece of mine involves insetting a pillar or taper in the center of a recycled glass punch bowl with a stabilizer in the bottom. The stabilizer is sometimes colored magical sand, black Witch's salt (powdered jet stone), or glass baubles. The candlelight glints beautifully off these embellishments. If you put an LED tea light atop a tall candleholder in the center of colored glass baubles or marbles, you can even serve Witch punch from the bowl (e.g., lemonade or limeade spiked with moonshine or vodka).

Alter your lighting decor to suit your tastes and to reflect each season's color changes and each Sabbat's magical meaning: Spiral holly or pine needles around candleholders at Yule. Surround them with flower buds at Beltane, or autumn leaves or acorns at Samhain. Cultivate helpful house brownies by meting cornmeal around

them. Set a pillar candle inside an antique silver bowl, fill clear round holiday orna-ments with reflective silver tinsel, recap them, and encircle the candle with them.[108]
You could also do the following:

* *Put a pillar atop a raised cake presentation plate.* When I arrive at a party, I frequently erect such a centerpiece on the spot in the center of the snack table. I add a fine bottle of wine nearby and arrange candles and sprinkle truffles and other delicate chocolates or candied fruits around it. The creative possibilities for these portable altar-type centerpieces are endless!

* *Use a wooden bowl from a thrift store.* Black, gray, beige, or plain wooden bowls filled with variously colored smooth river stones and with interspersed, inexpensive white or beeswax votive candles in glass holders in the center promote a tranquil, Zen-like ambience.

* *Some folk convert old colored bell-shaped tempered glass insulators once used atop telephone poles into candleholders.* These come in jewel colors such as red, green, yellow, and blue. I have seen some wrapped with wire around their threads, with a votive or tea lights inside, and hung from porch ceilings. They are charming and inviting above a porch swing.

You can always embellish the outside of a humdrum holder by using permanent marker or paint, or twirling a strand of gem chips around it. Sometimes rugged is best, and sometimes you have to gild the lily.

CANDLE SPELLS

"A CHILD'S birthday cake, with a candle on it for each year of life, points straight to one facet of the symbolism of candles.

A lighted candle, as a single source of light, is a single fragment of the universe's store of light, stands for an individual person's life as a single fragment of life in the world."

—Richard Cavendish, *Man, Myth and Magic*

---

108 Tinsel-filled ornaments also make goodly inexpensive Witch balls to gift or to hang in windows to avert the Evil Eye.

GYPSY CANDLE-FLIPPING SPELL

Belgian gypsies[109] purportedly worked this magic to avoid jail. Witches these days often do it to banish or repel. Use the spell during a new or waning moon night when you would spell to avoid court, win in court, or prevent or rid yourself of something or someone that you don't want.

Heat a boline or butter knife blade in hot tap water. Use it to cut off a portion of wax from the bottom of a candle, exposing the wick. Discard the excess wax, or save it as a *katharmata* offering to the Goddess Hecate.[110]

Powder myrrh resin and light it as incense. Face North. Burn the candle bottom side up in a candleholder while visualizing yourself worry-free of threat or concern.

CEROMANCY CANDLE DIVINATION

Pagans see the similarity between candle wax and semen, menstrual flow, and sexual climax fluid.

Ceromancy is the olde way of interpreting the way wax melts and heeding the magical meaning of the symbols that spilled or melted wax forms.

Always carefully observe how your candles generally melt in order to discern Elemental influences that are operative on present matters:

Drippy: Water	**Runny:** Water
Brittle: Air	**Spattery:** Water
Fast-drying: Air	**Spindly:** Air
Hard: Earth	**Sticky:** Water
Hot: Fire	**Stubby:** Earth
Mixed results: Fire or Water	**Wet:** Water

---

109 *Candle Lighting Encyclopedia*, Tina Ketch, Boaz Printing, Inc., 1991.
110 Spell in *The Goodly Spellbook*. Essentially, you bring ritual remains to a triple crossroad at night, appeal to Hecate for aid or thank Her for a boon, and then put your offering atop the ground and leave without turning back.

But if you would scry about something *specific*, spill some hot wax into a bowl of ice-cold water and keenly note the shape the wax assumes. Typically, wax in a color that contrasts with the vessel's color is easiest to read in detail, such as black wax in a water-filled white bowl, or white wax in a black bowl.

Since dried wax is fragile and difficult to keep intact, document symbols that seem particularly apt to what you're thinking or are worried about by taking a picture of the wax or drawing it in your personal Book of Shadows.

PROSPERITY CHARM

Lack feels like being sore oppressed by the restrictive planet Saturn, so break the cycle of poverty by repeatedly intoning the name of a planet God with attributes *opposite* to dour Saturn.

When you feel the bitter bite of want, on a Friday at sunset dye raw rice with green food coloring. While it air-dries, choose a candle color to burn. It can be coin-colored gold or silver, earthy green that magically corresponds with leprechauns, or royal blue or purple, sacred to the generous God Jupiter.

Dress the candle with gold leaf readily available at arts-and-crafts or home improvement stores and online venues. Sprinkle the magically "fixed" rice around the base of the candleholder. Burn plentiful oregano herb as incense.

Face the North direction and light your conjuring candle. Focus on the concept of holistic prosperity—being healthy, wealthy, peaceful, strong, and joyful. Visualize the abundance of the multi-universes replacing your dearth with success in all your pursuits.

Chant Jupiter's many names 30 times:

"JUPITER JOVE DEUS.
JUPITER-AMON ZEUS."

*

Thou will be charmed lucky!

ALTERNATIVE: Chant for aid from four Goddesses of plenty 30 times:

"LAKSHMI COPIA
ABUNDANTIA EUTHENIA"

TO PROTECT YOURSELF

At midnight on a Saturday, face the North and burn a foul-smelling aversion herb such as mugwort or asafetida and a black candle that represents known and unknown ill intent and the personal boundary that you will erect to protect yourself and/or your family or loved ones.

Put a red brick in a plastic bag and put it inside a paper bag, then pulverize it into dust using a rubber mallet or hammer. Mix equal amounts of bits of melted black wax, pulverized jet stone, and brick dust together and sprinkle it in a continuous line on the ground in front of your entrance door. It will repel from your premises folk who mean you ill or have the capacity to steal from you or harm you.

CANDLE UNCROSSING SPELL

When someone "works roots" on you, curses you up close (by shooting you the Evil Eye or "starring daggers at you" in "if looks could kill" fashion), or if they jinx you from afar, most folk know it.

Being jinxed feels *worse* than being under a dark cloud or experiencing an occasional string of ill luck: Its effects appear dire, relentlessly malevolent, and worsen over time versus improve or dissipate. Specific symptoms are classic, textbook even, and typically feature: sudden bizarre illnesses; loss of home, job, money, mate, and transport; discord with relatives and neighbors; gratuitous setbacks; and a sense of being crushed by picayune, daily, complicated problems. The combination of difficulties seems insurmountable because the issues continue to multiply.

Although there are many "de-jinxing" spells (for example, we include some ancient effective ones in *The Goodly Spellbook*), here is a 1970's vintage American one that features the kind of rudimentary rhyme that abounded during that era.

The following spell was found in a personal Book of Shadows used by one of *Diuvei's immediate family members. Its source is *Helping Yourself with White Witchcraft*, by Al G. Manning (Parker Publishing Co. Inc., West Nyack, NY, 1972). I give the spell as writ by the hand of the reader:

Put near under candle.[111] Pour a few drops of uncrossing oil on candle.[112] Light candle.

---

111 This refers to the rhyme spell below the preamble; it is implied that the rhyme be either written on parchment or intoned during the spell, or both. Candle color unspecified; I advise red to represent your magical goal of pushing back against the jinx with fiery force. Circle Quarter direction in which to face while performing the spell unspecified; I advise facing South (anger), with North having your back to support you banishing the curse.
112 Recipe for "uncrossing oil" unspecified: I advise extracting Dill weed in mineral oil for 21 days or so, then straining the spice from the liquid and using the resulting oil.

"FIRE AND OIL, NOW DO YOUR BEST,
UNCROSS AND FREE ME WITH GREAT ZEST.
SALAMANDERS, ZEPHYRS TRUE,
GNOMES AND TROLLS, AND UNDINES, TOO.
YOUR MIGHTY POWERS WORK FOR ME,
UNCROSSING AS YOU SET ME FREE.
SUCCESS AND POWER NOW TO ME,
AND AS MY WILL, SO MOTE IT BE."

TO FEEL PEACEFUL

As needed, sit in the West direction and cool your ire about a situation by immersing both hands in cold, sea-scented water inside a silver bowl.[113] Or you can burn one or more blue candles in the West or on a tub's rim while enjoying a soothing warm bath whose water is scented with dried lavender, chamomile, sage, or a combination thereof. If you lack these herbs or desire differently, substitute dried oats or olive, hemp, or mineral oil scented as you please.

Meditate on magical mysteries or Pagan paradoxes or sing or intone magical things that you're trying to memorize, such as God/dess names, power chants, or Barbarous Words in *The Goodly Spellbook*.

TO BECOME PSYCHIC

On a Monday after sunset, don clean white or purple clothing, anoint your "third eye" (on the forehead between your eyes) with lotus or eucalyptus oil, and wear a crystal pendant or wrap it around your left wrist. Stand in the center of a circle space or lie on your back in bed while burning a lunar silver or spirit purple candle.

Alternatively, sit facing the West direction while burning and scrying a Strega fire—lit alcohol poured atop Epsom salts in a cauldron or a fire-resistant container.

Acquire the skill by relaxing versus stressing about or forcing it. Gently focus on seeing events from afar—of folk you know and those you don't. If you push aught, may it be in the distance afar that you encourage your mind's eye to see. Witness goodly things as well as unseemly happenings. Encourage yourself to simply witness, not judge or try to affect the outcome.

---

113 This spell variation is also goodly for dealing with bad bosses, mean mates, negative neighbors, petty despots, and so forth.

After the exercise, sleep, bathe, or do other self-soothing things.

Ignore perceived failures or your initial inability to replicate your capacities each and every time; rather, write, record, or log and reward your progress.

TO TRANCE OUT

To aspire to great heights of mind, start deep.

After sunset on a Friday, dress in dark clothing, anoint yourself with myrrh oil, and burn a brown candle in the North. Set your spirit free by listening to Witchy-Pagani or world music and dancing increasingly uninhibitedly. Spin wildly to the beat and stomp to agree with lyrics that touch your heart. In short, loose yourself in movement.

Whirl around a prop such as a cape, shawl, silk scarf, or sash or twirl a wand or a pair of practice swords—anything you wish so long as it's enabling versus distracting. Dance till you're pleasantly exhausted. Eat a bite to replenish your blood sugar and then record your insights or epiphanies.

TO REMEMBER OR AFFECT YOUR DREAMS

Lucid dreaming can be disconcerting at first, because some dreams are unpleasant or downright frightening. Yet as with divination, it's better to know and honestly remember dreams and consider their content meaning than to remain in the dark. 'Tis a goodly way to truly know thyself.

On a Monday night, secrete an infinity symbol resembling a horizontal number eight in or under your pillowcase, insert earplugs, and prior to sleep, burn a white sea-scented votive candle. Or you can skip the earplugs and burn the candle while listening to ocean sounds. You'll remember more and experience fewer headaches if the head of your bed is facing in the North direction.

Keep a voice-activated digital recorder beside your bed to encourage you to dictate all impressions as soon as you can remember them—whether it be upon waking, shortly thereafter, or as they intrude on your mind during the day. Track patterns and trends and learn to note minute differences such as God/dess input versus your inner fears or desires or as the weather or your life circumstances change.

TO BE HEALTHY

On a Sunday at noon, burn in the South direction a solar gold candle (to heal a non-feverish condition or illness), an orange one (to increase energy), or a yellow one (to warm up the cold and weak).[114] For extra magical punch, burn some sunny yellow frankincense or tree sap amber or copal resin incense. Intone the olde "Three Ladies" charm to take the sting out or use the Boneset spell in *The Goodly Spellbook*.

SUN STRENGTH SPELL

When you feel hard beset, at noon on a Sunday burn dragon's blood incense and light two orange tapers. Stand facing the South direction. Spread your legs apart until your hips feel centered and then spread your arms out wide away from your torso.

While holding a burning candle in each hand, intone this Latin quatrain nine times:

> "SOL ET SULIS LUCEANT SUPER ME. QUOD QUASI GLADIUM
> ACTUM ET MEA OPERA."

[Sol and Sulis shine on me. Strong as a sharp sword make my deeds.]
When you feel goodly energized, dip a coin in the melted wax and carry the talisman in your pocket or purse to provide you courage, strength, and will.

TO DIVINE YOUR LIFE SPAN

Although some folk claim that they would shudder in horror to learn when they will die, just as many pine to know so that they would more readily relish life, get their affairs in order, and express heartfelt sentiments to loved ones before they succumb.

To discern if you will live through the coming year, face the East at midnight on Samhain, light antiseptic-scented incense such as lotus or eucalyptus, and try to completely burn down a white candle. If the candle melts wholly down, your prospects for survival are promising! If it goes out before being fully liquefied, however, slow down, be more temperate in your choices and actions, and take aggressive prophylactic magical measures to maximize your health and safety, such as working protection spells.

ALTERNATIVE: Burn candles in a menorah. The candelabra's branches represent the Tree of Life and the seven planets that influence everyone on a daily basis.

---

114 Lighting a brown candle could invoke a slow recovery with complications; green, promote infection; red, spike a fever; white, encourage stroke; purple, induce a coma; or black, draw the Grim Reaper.

Stare at the holder and, going from left to right, mentally assign each candle to represent a rough time frame; for instance, the first candle on your left could signify from Samhain to Yule or Imbolc or something similar.

Note how all the candles melt as a group—consistently or randomly—as well as the time line individual candles represent. Do they gutter, sputter, extinguish themselves, or burn too aggressively? Does one flame burn tall but another one squat near the wick's base? Do the candles drip excessively, implying copious mourning weeping, or does their wax seem intent on pooling in place around the wick, symbolizing bodily intactness?

Interpret your omens by using basic magical correspondences theory, but generally, active and stable flames bode well and vocal or wispy candles portend ill.

TO DETERMINE IF SOMEONE WILL RECOVER FROM ILLNESS, INJURY, OR SURGERY

It can be agonizing for Craft clergy, Coven members, family, friends, and survivors to watch sick folk suffer overlong from an intractable condition that refuses to loosen its grip and provide the ill with the Gods' ease of sorrow's end.

To see if death shadows someone, on a Saturday night at midnight during a waning or new moon, face the North direction and burn incense associated with death rites, such as myrrh. Then enflame a black candle and intently scry its flame: If it is a "guttering candle"[115]—lights with difficulty, sputters weakly, or puts itself out—the answer is "yes," so prepare yourself to deal with the person's imminent or inevitable demise gracefully.

TO ATTRACT A LOVER

On a Friday after sunset, face the South. Write down in minute detail exactly what you want, personality aspects that you don't want, what you can live with and possibly forgive, and what you cannot abide in any circumstances. When you're sure you've thought of every positive attribute and every negative potential, light patchouli, musk, or civet cat incense and bind two candles tightly together—one orange (representing the desirable energy signals you're sending) and one red (representing a sensual mate). Burn them upright.

---

115 *Cavendish, Man, Myth and Magic: An Illustrated Encyclopedia of the Supernatural*, Vol. 14, BPC Publishing Ltd./Petty and Sons Ltd., Leeds and London, 1970.

To attract long-lasting companionship, light copal incense and bind together with a brown string or ribbon one pink candle representing your desire for platonic love and one blue candle for the compassionate friendship you want. Burn.

While working either spell, visualize having happy experiences with the person and intone the contents of your list followed by saying passionate conjuring words or tangible promises of friendship.

FERTILI-TREE SPELL

Conjure conception by bedecking a tree with spring "pysanky." This word refers to the Russian magic custom of drizzling eggshells with molten wax, and then dyeing them and chipping off the wax to reveal gorgeous patterns.

INGREDIENTS:

Clear glass vase	Plastic bowls
Cooking pot	Scissors, egg-piercing, sharp
Dyes	String
Fresh eggs	Twiggy tree
Paraffin or wax	Water

At night during a spring waxing moon, weight the bottom of a vase with water. Snip a twiggy portion of a tree that branches out like an open hand. Vertically insert it into the vase. Pierce the eggs and blow out/drain their contents. Save the liquid to cook and consume. Put the shells in dye bowls.

Moisten various natural dyes such as food coloring, coffee grounds, or crushed laundry bluing. Put them in their own bowl. Melt a bit of paraffin or wax in a pot atop a stove burner. Use a chopstick or whatnot to drizzle it onto the eggs. Let the wax air-dry.

Gently roll each shell around in its dye bowl. Let it air-dry. Remove the wax to reveal the egg's negative, undyed design. Glue strings to egg holes and decorate the tree with the ornaments. As the tree buds, so will you be fruitful!

ALTERNATIVES: Suspend the eggs from hand tie-dyed string or substitute colorful embroidery floss.

TO KNOW IF A LOVER IS FAITHFUL

Burn a brown candle outside, near where your loved one lives. If the flame inclines toward you, your loved one is devoted and true; if not, the person is faithless.[116]

TO WIN A LOVER BACK

Anoint a red candle with musk oil, light it, and then thrust two straight pins through its burning wick.[117]

TO MAKE A KEY DECISION

On a Wednesday at noon, face the East direction, don clinically cold yellow citrine or agate, and anoint your forehead with lotus oil. Burn a yellow candle while deeply pondering the detriments of your dilemma. Ask the God/desses to give you a definitive omen regarding which choice to make, and when They do, act as Their input guides you.

TO LEARN SECRET MOTIVATION

On a Monday at midnight face the East direction and burn three candles: one black, representing the secret; one red, symbolizing your ire at those conspiring to keep the secret from you; and one purple to represent the spirit of the secret, whose nature is to strive to be revealed. The speed at which each burns reveals all. For instance, if the black one burns longest, the secret is truly potentially damaging to you; if the red burns longest, it's decidedly personal, dangerous, and hateful; and if the purple burns longest, you have hope of vindicating yourself from the wrongful lies and rumors that abound about you.

TO STOP STRIFE

On a Friday after sunset, face the East direction. Fill a clear glass container with cold water. Light and hold a white candle in your left hand. While slowly spinning an odd number of times ayenward (widdershins/counterclockwise), verbally banish Roudmo (a spirit of discord) by repeatedly intoning His name backward—"Omdour"—nine times each in seven incremental directions that invisibly divide the circle. In other

---

116 Ibid.
117 One pin represents you, the other, a "poppet" prick of your desired one. Obviously you should also verbally and physically express your desire in spellwork with the supportive spell provided in *The Goodly Spellbook*.

words, stand in the circle and spin your body leftward, stopping at each Quarter and semi-Quarter and say what you will about the matter. When you feel the time is right, drip the candle into the cold water while appealing to the harmony Goddess Concordia or the peace God Pax and then turn the candle upside down and quench the flame in the water.

TO INCLINE COOPERATION

On a Wednesday after sunset, face the West direction and promote equanimity by burning a gray or silver-colored candle sacred to Mercury, a God of communication. Burn a softly scented incense such as rose or honeysuckle and either a white candle (to show your pure intent *sans* a personal agenda, simply your desire to accomplish something for the greater good), a pink candle (to attract folk to you and your cause), a red candle (to impress your compatriots with a sense of urgency about their need to enable you), or a brown candle (to make their help resolute and sustained). Folks will feel that you are non-confrontational and will reciprocate reasonably.

TRADITIONAL WAX PENTACLE

Witches have craftily survived eons of persecution of our religious practices, in part because of our long history of making magical tools from molten wax. This way, if a threat presents, we can pitch the tools into a fire and quickly eliminate incriminating evidence of our spellwork. This trick also works to foil nosy landlords, relatives, or neighbors.

Make a traditional round wax pentacle for your main altar—yellow if it's Eastern, green if Northern, or red, green, yellow, and blue if you have an altar in each of the four directions.

INGREDIENTS:

New or used colored taper candles	Water
Lipped baking sheet	Stove
Wax paper	Wick-fishing implement
Two nesting cooking pots (double boiler setup)	Bowl
	Boline or butter knife

On a Wednesday evening, place the baking sheet on a flat surface and line it with wax paper. Drape some excess beyond all sides to form lifting handles. Set aside an extra sheet of wax paper. Half fill the large pot with water and place it on a stove burner to boil. Balance the small uncovered pot inside the large pot.

Melt one candle color at a time in the small pot. When liquid, quickly remove wicks with tongs or a chopstick or whatnot and air-dry flat atop the extra sheet of wax paper. Quickly pour the melted wax into the lipped baking sheet, covering the entire bottom to each side, about ¼ inch (6mm) deep.

When cool to the touch but not yet dry, turn the bowl upside down in the middle of the wax and use the boline or a butter knife wet in hot water to trace around its rim and form the wax round. Bigrave the pentacle with traditional Gardnerian glyphs, a sentiment written in a magical alphabet, astrological signs, Elemental triangles, or other sacred sigils such as pentagrams, spirals, and crescents. When dry, use the wax paper handles to lift the wax off the baking sheet. Trim design if desired, remove wax paper backing, and put the wax paten in a place of honor in your circling space.

HAND OF GLORY SPELL

I recommend being a Witch proud of Paganism's merits, but if for some reason you would cloak, obscure, or hide your spellwork, on a Saturday at midnight use an olde burglar trick that prevented interruption of their nefarious deeds.

Rough justice prevailed for eons, so for a long time hangings, public executions, grave robbing, and body parts displayed on pikes were commonplace, easily enabling thieves to acquire a dead man's hand.

Burglars would target a place to pilfer, erect their macabre collected fingers upright inside a candelabra, and set the digits alight. The finger fat burned like candlewicks, as seen in the original movie *The Wicker Man*.

These days you can finger-form a hand candle from semi-cool paraffin or melted wax and enclose a wick in each fingertip. Or you can buy a molded one from an online occult supply store or seasonal Halloween shop. The one I keep in the ritual room on my North Quarter altar melted in a way that made it seem that there was bone beneath its outer wax "flesh."

ALTERNATIVE: Mimic the scent of decay in a hand that you make by adding a noxious herb such as asafetida or mugwort to the melted wax.

Or you can dress a purchased hand with death-scented oil. Infuse olive oil with peat moss, oven-dried fresh mushrooms, or the like. When ready to use, strain the oil of plant matter and label and date the contents.

TO WREAK RIGHTEOUS REVENGE

Vengeance need not equate with hostility on your part: All people sense when they're disliked, ill-treated, or threatened, and since Witches are well meaning, it's only fair that by word, deed, and magic we repulse attack or injustice when the need arises.

This spell's timing can vary with the specific nature of the situation. Sometimes you counter by using the same Element that the attack involves, whereas at other times you use its opposite. For instance, if it's a verbal attack or injustice, you could do it on a Wednesday, the day of communication and legality; if it's a nefarious sneak attack, in the darkness of a Saturday night.

If it's a physical threat, you could fight fire with fire by working on a Sunday evening or, oppositely, quench their ire by casting the spell on a cooling lunar Monday. Use your best instinct regarding magical correspondences; you can always repeat the spell using a different Element until it takes hold and yields the result you seek.

After sunset, face the North direction and burn a noxiously scented incense and a black candle: Both represent the wrongdoer. Next, light a white candle to represent justice. Visualize yourself surrounded by an impenetrable protective pentagram and, extending beyond its magic bubble, a thorny, electric, or similarly inviolate boundary line. Imbibe bitter tea. Appeal to vengeance entities and deities to magically defend you by heaping the offender with such incessant ill luck that he or she becomes contrite and compassionate. Examples include the following:

Andraste	Lilith
Ares	Mars[118]
Fates	Pluto
Furies	Sekhmet
Grandmother Spider	Sobek
Hades	Zeus
Hecate	
Kali-Ma	

---

118 In His latter martial aspect. Originally, He was a beneficient garden God.

If the white candle burns better than the black, your plight has been heard and you'll be avenged.

Sip something sweet such as honey-mead during Cakes & Wine afterward and thank the Gods in advance by pouring some as an offering adoors.

DURING A RITE FOR THE DEPARTED SOUL

Preferably on a Monday or Friday night, if the deceased is a Gardnerian Initiate, burn the remainder of the pair of red candles burned when the beloved dead attained first-, second-, or third-degree magical rank. If the dearly departed was a non-Initiated Pagan, burn three: one black in the North, equating with death; one purple in the center of the circle, honoring the Element Spirit; and one white in the East, representing reincarnation.

Intone the words from the rite in the traditional Book of Shadows or anything from your heart. Make a widdershins circuit: Mourn their passing in the North, extol their virtues in the West, recount their foibles in the South, and ask the God/desses to welcome them into the Witches' afterlife—the Summerlands—so they may rest before reincarnating and reuniting with their Covenmates or being embraced by Pagan folk of like mind.

Consume Cakes & Wine in their honor and leave some adoors to appease their Spirit if it could be "hungry" (i.e., died angry or frustrated).

While many these days upload a memorial web page, online is not exactly a touchy-feely place to go during grief. Rather, erect an ancestor shrine in their honor in the North direction on a wee wall cabinet, bookshelf, windowsill, or in your ritual room. Decorate it with candle bits from the Departed Soul ritual, pictures of them inside miniature frames, and/or tokens of them such as their business card, signature, a swatch from their favorite clothes, a piece of their jewelry, or a heat-felt poem about them that you composed, etc. When in need of their aid, approach the altar and request that they send you a guiding omen. Every annual Samhain Sabbat (Halloween), keep their spirit at peace with an offering of a sweet or an honoring, empty place setting at a traditional Dumb Supper consumed in contemplative silence.

REMOVING WAX FROM CANDLES

I've taught for decades that 99% of what a real Witch does is "scrape wax" because removing the malleable substance can be a messy business. Dried wax tends to smear and resists removal by the universal solvent water and by degreasing liquid dishwashing soap as well.

I practice what I preach, for even as I wrote this, I had to break off and clean a dozen different types of candleholders after our most recent public Samhain Sabbat in our Covenstead.

Several were of liquid-molded starburst glass; one was a tall, intricately detailed copper taper holder minutely engraved in a bark and leaves motif; several were silver; and there was one that the High Priest had roughly sand-cast when a child, in silvery Frankenmetal alloy.

The glass was sooty, slippery, and fragile; the copper, a nightmare to tackle because of its intricate carving; and the silver, a challenge to prevent permanently scratching and to dry without encouraging tarnish. On top of the latters' innate challenge, the metal holder's roughness fought to cleave to the wax, yet I patiently persisted and cleaned them all to pristine status by scraping them with a blunt metal kitchen knife beneath über-hot water, soaking them for some minutes in dishwashing liquid, and repeat rinse-scrubbing them beneath more hot water.

Wax removal can be a tedious process, so I prefer to approach it as an opportunity to work magic. As I "do the voodoo," I take heed of any omens revealed in the images that the remaining blobs or candle drippings formed, relish the memory of the magical event that created the chaos, "wax off" with purposefully widdershins scraping and rubbing motions, and take pride in starting fresh with a clean slate. I think many things, creating solutions to problems or challenges that I may be anticipating or experiencing at the time.

You can use a boline, a disposable blunt plastic knife, or a cleanable metal butter knife to remove big blobs and teensy wax or soot splatters from altars, metal pots, wooden tables, and the like, and then cover the affected surface with a towel saturated in hot water. When the remains have loosened, go over the area with Dawn™, wood wax, or whatever it takes to make the affected surface pristine again.

CANDLE AND TAROT SPELLS

Tarot cards reveal past and future events and present influences based on the mystical meanings of color and Element correspondences; imagery details; number theory; astrological symbols; alphabet letter meanings, such as Hebrew; the overall shape that a card image resembles (oval, diamond, etc.); and the position in which the cards appear when drawn from the deck and laid down on a flat surface (upright or reversed).

Playing cards can be used in lieu of tarot because their numerical and suit meanings reflect those of their more intricate predecessor.

The meanings, correspondences, and magical uses of the Elements, planets, and many symbols are explained and illustrated in "The Goodly," and the section "Arithmomancy: Number Divination" provides a cheat sheet to reference when you are divining the future by reading playing cards.

I combine candles with cards when I read tarot for clients. When the querent[119] has no specific burning question, I light a candle and randomly pull a single "clue card" from the deck; I let the candle illuminate the card and keep the card's meaning as a focus in connection with the other cards in the full reading.

To work candle and card craft, select a candle whose color corresponds to your feeling, situation, or spell goal and place it to your left. Call it by your name or "the wronged party," "the injured person," and so forth—whatever's apt. Then remove from a tarot deck the card that most closely resembles you or the reason you're working the spell[120] and place it face up beneath the candleholder.

Place a second candle whose color corresponds to your problem or wish on your right. Call it your spell target's name or issue words. Place beneath its holder a different tarot card whose meaning resembles the way you want the issue to be resolved in your favor.

To attract something or someone, burn the candles a bit while visualizing and spelling over them and then move them closer together over minutes, days, or weeks until they touch or your spell comes to fruition, whichever happens first.

To banish or repel something, do the same thing, only space the candles farther apart over time until they can no longer "see" themselves in the same room or you know that the threat has abated.

---

119 The inquirer of the cards; the person receiving a card reading.
120 This is called the significator card.

Another satisfying candle/tarot spell is to purposefully select cards to illustrate a story that ends in the way that you want your problem to resolve. For instance, if you're exhausted by moving too much, you wouldn't spell for stability by picking the Fool card as part of your spell story because it depicts a naïve traveler; nor should you choose the Tower card, which sports a lightning-struck citadel on fire. Instead, you might pick an Earthy pentacle card whose numbers equate with a stable home, such as the 4 or 8 of Pentacles symbolizing walls or the 10 meaning completion as in a furnished home that won't require a lot of maintenance or repair.

You can also use melted candle wax as glue to fuse the cards together in a stack in the order in which they occur in telling the story. Secrete the lot beneath an altar cloth to enable them to work your will at their leisure.

Or you can use melted candle wax to affix a written scroll atop a card that represents your spell desire.

These basic magical methods can be altered in an infinite variety of spell permutations that vary according to your spell timing; what your magical spell intention is; what candle color and card you pick; the issue you have; the kinds of words or chanted charms you use, such as powerful Barbarous Words in an unknown tongue; what magical oil or incense you use to support the rest of your spell ingredients; and so forth.

TAROT CANDLE GIFT

Pour melted wax into a recycled jar with a central wick or three. When it sets dry, put clear epoxy glue on the side of a tarot card that doesn't sport traditional imagery and affix it onto the outside of the jar as decor. If the card resists lying flat against the glass, put tight rubber bands around the card and glass to achieve a goodly seal. For instance, if a friend needs healing, you could use the Sun card. Witchy insight? The Moon. Money? The 10 of Pentacles, and so forth.

CANDLE AND RUNE SPELLS

Female Witches take to the tarot, whereas male Witches run for the runes. Runic is an olde magical alphabet illustrated in *The Goodly Spellbook*. Runes for divination are each inscribed with one of these letters and most commonly come in rectangular tile form, most oft sold in carved wood, bone, stone, or ceramic.

Runes can take time to master because much of their original meaning and cultural context was lost after years of conquerors slaughtering and Christians repressing the Nordic Pagan tribal folk who used them.

To work candle-rune spells, ask your question, randomly remove one rune from the rune pouch, and let its meaning dictate the color of the spell candle that you will burn to resolve an issue. The meaning of the rune may be beneficent—predicting goodly luck or victory and the like—so you know to choose a "light" color that most closely corresponds with its traditional meaning. Another rune may warn or discourage a plan, so you would opt for a darker candle.

Or you can burn a purple candle and ask the Goddess Iris of the rainbow bridge[121] to have the Gods guide you to select the specific rune that will reveal crucial information or details about your problem or the way to resolve it. Then randomly pull one and interpret its meaning.

Or you can think about your dilemma and ask a yes/no question about it. Select a rune at random and lay it before a lit white candle near a breeze or draft. Watch as its wax melts into phantasmagoric shapes and then scrutinize the candle. Your answer is "Yes" if the result resembles the rune but "No" if it is plainly opposite the sigil. Your answer is equivocal if it is illegible or if you cannot see any particular correlation between the wax and the rune inscription. In this case, reformulate your question to be more specific, ask it aloud, and watch for your sign to appear.

RUNE CANDLE GIFT

Pour melted candle wax into a recycled jar with a central wick or three tied vertically onto a pencil balancing atop the vessel. While letting it set firmly, take a smidge of self-hardening clay and finger-form a small square, rectangle, or roundel atop wax paper.

Before the clay shape dries completely, bigrave a rune atop it that corresponds to what you want your friend to get or keep, such as a home (the Odal rune), and then use a skewer or something similar to punch through a hole near its top.

When all's dry, scissor-snip the wick(s) off the pencil about 1/8 inch (3mm) above the top of the wax and then snake a ribbon, lace, hempen string, or something similar through the rune's hole and tightly tie the rune around the upper lip or rim of the jar.

---

121 The precursor of the communication God Mercury, Iris carries messages between the Gods and humans.

GLASS RUNE SET MAKING SPELL

INGREDIENTS:

    25 oval colored glass vase reflectors

    Paint pen

    Rune pouch

    Candle, salt water, and incense

On a Wednesday after sunset paint each rune with a runic alphabet letter, leaving one blank. Air-dry, put the runes in a pouch of your choice, and then consecrate the set before reading with it. Cast circle, light incense and a candle, and then anoint the pouch with salt water and pass it briefly through the incense smoke and candle flame. Verbally charge the set to read accurately for you and then make your first pull from the bag.

LEATHER RUNE SET MAKING SPELL

INGREDIENTS:

    A flat piece of black or brown leather

    Scissors or a box cutter

    Silver or green paint pen

    Ruler

    Rune pouch of choice

    Candle, salt water, and incense

On a Saturday at midnight, lay the leather rough side upward on a flat, stable surface. Use the ruler to measure and the pen to draw cut marks—vertical stripes with evenly spaced gaps between them. Then turn the leather at a right angle and draw more vertical stripes until you have an even check pattern of at least 25 rectangles. Your runes will be the size between the stripes, so measure according to your preference; however, a goodly lightweight, portable size for a rune set is 1 inch (2.54cm) by 1 inch (2.54cm) or even thumbnail size.

Use the scissors or a box cutter to cut out your runes. Then turn the leather smooth side upward, and if it's black, paint each soft tile with one of the traditional 24 runic sigils with silver paint; if it is brown, use green. Leave one tile unadorned, blank. It's a "wild card" that means equivocal, "ask again later," or the Gods are mum on the subject.

Air-dry the tiles and then place them in your bag. The bag can be leather, velvet, or organza—whatever you want to make or buy. Cast circle, light incense and a candle, and then anoint the bag with salt water and pass it briefly through the incense smoke and candle flame. Tell the runes what you expect of them to read truly to you, and then make your first random pull.

ALTERNATIVE: Instead of consecrating the set with altar Elements, take it adoors and expose it to air and earthy ground and then anoint the rune pouch with water and pass it briefly through flame.

WOOD RUNE SET MAKING SPELL

INGREDIENTS:

A dried wood limb a uniform 1 inch (2.54cm) by 1 inch
    (2.54cm) in diameter

Handsaw

Pencil

Electric wood-burning tool

Wax paper

A pair of work gloves (plastic or latex)

Tung oil

Rune pouch of choice

Find a dry limb on the ground and place it horizontally atop a stable, flat surface. Make vertical pencil marks across the limb's length, spaced ¼ inch (6mm) apart. Saw the cut marks to produce 25 round tiles for your set or more if you want to choose the best ones for your set from among many pieces.

Plug in your wood-burning tool. While you wait for it to heat up, use your pencil to draw a rune on each of 24 tiles. Leave one tile blank. Wood-burn the runes onto the tiles.

Next, tear off a piece of wax paper large enough to hold the rune set without the tiles touching. Don your gloves and then waterproof each rune by dipping it into natural tung oil (made of crushed beetle wings). Air-dry the runes atop the wax paper. Repeat with more coats of tung oil as desired to achieve a rich color and sheen.

Consecrate the set before use by exposing it to the Elements.

ALTERNATIVE: Use a bright green or silver-colored paint pen to make your wood-burned runes pop against the wood background, let them air-dry, and then preserve them in Tung oil.

TORCH MAGIC: PORTABLE FLAME

"What are thou Freedom?

For the labourer it is bread,

And a comely table spread.

Thou art clothes, and fire,

and food for the trampled multitude."

—Percy Shelley, English lyric Romantic poet

The original wildwood emerged from the last Ice Age. Ancient Pagans maximized their success not only by timing their hunting, planting, and traveling plans to coincide with the waxing moon and full moon but also by packing backups such as portable flint; a twisting stick, twine, and flat board; or a lit coal wrapped in damp grass and flammable fat, resin, or coal tar pitch[122] with which to fashion a fire or torches.

Our Ancestors crafted torches from bulrushes, cattails, reeds, seedpods, shrubbery, stalks, and tree limbs. They held them in hand to illuminate animal tracks, seed rows, paths, and streams. They waved them atop high places to communicate distress or warn of incoming marauders. They set them vertically in the ground as a protective perimeter around their sleeping sites to discourage carnivores.

Over some eons, people clear-cut brambles, manicured hedgerows to delineate property, and nurtured gnarly groves and pastures to accommodate grazing livestock and planting fields.

During the Anglo-Saxon era, wooded commons were owned by one but used by all: Typically, the lord owned the ground but commoners could let their animals graze the fields, and both lord and commoners harvested the wood for building and fire fuel, among other things.

---

122 Pitch was so prized that it stretches credulity to believe that castle refugees under siege routinely wasted the precious resource by pouring it by the bucketful onto the heads of enemies below their ramparts and lit it afire as movies oft depict.

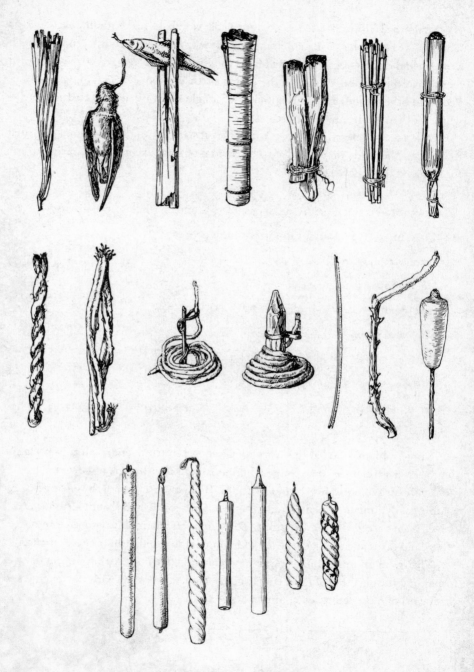

Medieval Europeans used many renewable woods to make torch poles, such as "coppice" (trees such as ash and elm that regrew from their stumps), "sucker" (such as aspen and cherry trees that cloned from their roots), and "pollard" (trees trimmed feet above the ground to reduce the eating of their shoots by grazing animals).[123] People in other climes availed themselves of jungle vine or dried braided seaweed— whatever their environment offered.

Olden terms referring to what "estover" (subsistence wood) that those relegated to living in the wilds were entitled to by custom or were exempt from having to pay for included the following:

Cartbote—wood used to make essential utensils, wheels, and so on

Chiminage—toll paid for going through a forest

Firebote—firewood

Hedgebote—fence wood

Housebote—wood to build a home

Lops and tops—fuel wood cut from old high tree growth

Piscary—right to make personal reed fish weirs

Turbary—right to cut fuel turf or peat

Vert and venison—right to harvest local wood and eat local game

King William, who led the Norman Conquest in 1066, ended all this by claiming the land as solely his own to sport hunt boar and deer that he imported.

Successive rulers were even more ruthless: They curried support by gifting extravagantly costly timber to toadies and, when strapped for cash to mount Crusades, sold nobles huge parcels of land for profit. To sycophants, their ability to rape resources offset land taxes and scutage (the fee a knight paid to avoid military participation).

The trend toward eliminating common land[124] continued with stringent decrees forbidding the gleaning of royal lands and concluded over time with the fencing and closing off of most countries' commons.

---

123 *The History of the Countryside*, Oliver Rackham, J. M. Dent and Sons, London, 1986.
124 Then called "afforestation" versus today's "deforestation."

This thrust many a widow, orphan, and poor family into dire straits because they could no longer legally use wood to cook with or warm themselves and were denied a sideline source of income from selling torch material.

These injustices sparked many a rebellion, such as that which, within less than 200 years after William the Conqueror, led to the Magna Carta agreement of 1215.

MAGNA CARTA, CHAPTER 47: *"All forests that have been made forest in our time shall be immediately disafforested; and so be it done with riverbanks that have been made preserves by us in our time."*[125]

CHAPTER 48: *"All evil customs connected with forests and warrens, foresters and warreners, sheriffs and their officials, river-banks and their wardens shall immediately be inquired into in each county by twelve sworn knights of the same county who are to be chosen by good men of the same county and within forty days of the completion of the inquiry shall be utterly abolished by them so as never to be restored. . . ."*

Although King John had the pact written[126] to appease mutinous nobles, he promptly disavowed the document, and Pope Innocent III supported him by issuing a papal bull declaring it null and void. By the next year both were dead within three months of each other—the Pope of fever and John of dysentery.

Prince Louis of France resolved the civil war between the French and English by reissuing the Magna Carta on September 11, 1217, and days later issuing a charter re-legalizing forest use by commoners.

The charters were reissued together in 1225, and the Yorkshire County rolls include the name of Robert Hod in 1226: Clearly, the famous outlaw Robin Hood flourished during the time of the Magna Carta.

Strictures remained, such as malignant penalties for actually gleaning wood. For example, if a cart was used to transport wood, it could be confiscated and sold; this had the natural effect of forcing folk to carry wood on their backs.

Later, when many American colonies sought to thwart English royalty by using Magna Carta language to compose their own charters, they nonetheless "ignored its forest provisions altogether when it came to their own intrusions into the woodlands."[127]

---

125 The Magna Carta's most far-reaching provisions aren't the ones most people were taught in school. "From Wildwood to Wooded Pasture to Political Forest," in Peter Linebaugh, "The Secret History of the Magna Carta," *Boston Review*, http://bostonreview.net/BR28.3/linebaugh.nclk.
126 Ibid. There is no evidence that King John was literate or signed the parchment.
127 Ibid.

When you wonder how nonpark forests became such a rarity or ponder how people became so alienated from the forest, know that it was through such series of punitive edicts that rendered folk who subsisted on renewable wood suspect, furtive, and outlawed.

Prize the Pagan love of the wildwood, of making love in a spring greenwood, and of fashioning magical fires. Flotsam and jetsam yet collect in urban corners. Be grateful that some torch material remains and can be bound to light our way. Let not the forest be relegated to fairy tales and virtual tours: Do much to conserve, protect, and perpetuate the benefits of torches.

HANDHELD TORCH-MAKING RECIPES

TRADITIONAL RESIN TORCH

Find on the ground a straight "green" (wet wood) tree branch that is 2 to 3 feet long and 2 to 3 inches (5.08 to 7.62cm) wide. Stripping bark off to make a handhold on greenwood is difficult and retaining the bark improves the hot grip, so leave the limb natural.

USE ORGANIC FUEL: Slather the top with sticky tree bark sap such as pine resin (melted copal incense). Air-dry before sparking. Your torch will take a minute or so to catch alight but can burn up to an hour—approximately the time it would take to illuminate outdoor storytelling or a touching magical ritual. Preferably add its last gasp to a rock-lined outdoor balefire pit; otherwise, snuff it out in stream water, by tossing a wet towel over it, or by rolling it on the ground in dry dirt.

ALTERNATIVES: Substitute as a natural accelerant beeswax or outdoor-cooked leftover animal or bacon fat.

CLOTHESLINE ACCELERANT TORCH

Find on the ground a straight "green" (wet wood) tree branch that is 2 to 3 feet long and 2 to 3 inches (5.08 to 7.62cm) wide. Keep the bark intact. Wrap non-dyed cotton clothesline rope around the top of the torch so that you create a mid-bulge, and secure it by tucking the last bit beneath the main body.

Use a nonnatural accelerant: Fully saturate the fabric with torch fuel or a similar accelerant. Any non-saturated bit may toast and ash away in the air. Keep it away from fire, kids, and pets for a minimum of two hours while you let it air-dry and off-gas.

Set the tip ablaze. The torch can burn up to an hour to serve as a woodland light or rite decor.

ALTERNATIVES: Substitute a Y-shaped stick. Use the lower vertical end as a handle, and then loop clothesline in and around its Y branches in an infinity symbol/figure 8 pattern. Substitute for a stick a wood dowel available at home improvement stores.

Substitute cotton T-shirt material, socks, or rags for the clothesline.

FUEL TIPS AND SAFE SETTING

When Witches don't make our own torches, we often substitute tabletop-size rattan tikis or tall ones for setting in soil.

Tall tiki torches have a bamboo stake with a woven wood strip cup on top to house a fuel canister insert. You can most cost-effectively acquire tiki torches off-season during autumn and wintertime, at online party sites, or at brick-and-mortar gardening, hardware, or home improvement stores; their price soars during the outdoor entertaining spring and summer seasons.

The best tall tikis include a safe, durable metal torch-fuel canister instead of an inexpensive, transparent plastic insert whose sole virtue can be a reduction in over-filling because you can see the fuel line as it rises.

A goodly tall tiki should also include a primitive bamboo flame snuffer tied to the outside of the fuel cup. When the fuel canister insert is removed for transport to a ritual site, the snuffer can be dropped inside the cup to prevent breakage.

I don't recommend burning cheap kerosene in tikis, as it reeks and produces copious amounts of sooty smoke. Rather, burn fuel specific to torches that is widely available in most grocery stores because many use it to power indoor hurricane lamps; however, the minimal bottle amount in which these fuels typically sell is more expensive than that offered off-season in bulk in hardware and home improvement stores. Some brands are even formulated to burn in a specific color: I favor blue, which is breathtaking in moonlight.

Transport each torch-fuel canister insert empty and with its wick upright, preferably with each canister inside its own box in a recycled cardboard beverage six-pack carrier.

If you need to transport many tikis for an outdoor ritual, stabilize multiple carriers inside an empty heavy plastic milk bottle crate. The hand opening on each side of it enables easy toting from car to woodland grove.

Line a separate plastic milk bottle crate with a cardboard box to soak up fuel drips and then fill it with a torch-setting kit. It should contain the following:

* Diverse sharp objects such as a long screwdriver, a chisel, a claw hammer, and a spade to enable you to pierce hard-packed earth or frozen ground

* A tarp to protect the grass or ground from contamination by dripped fuel.

* A large plastic funnel to use to fill the canisters with fuel.

* A metal skewer or two to help you poke the wicks up through the opening if they fall down into the canister.

* A skein of hemp or a roll of twine to bind together any stake that splits during setting.

* Rags or a canister of wet wipes to remove fuel from your hands.

* Something to mark where you want to set the torches.

Since we often set dozens of tikis at a time to delineate the boundary and directional orientation of a huge outdoor circle, we often mark our torch placement plans by using dozens of bright orange plastic flags with thin metal posts.

I've learned that although the flags are ugly and utilitarian, their points are sharp and can normally penetrate the ground with the pressure from only one hand and project upward, making them easy to see. Small or flat items are difficult to see and easy to leave behind on a grassy field after dark.

When you're afield, set your markers so that the circle or torch arrangement looks aesthetically pleasing and geometrically even say, circular versus raggedy lopsided). Then lay the tarp down flat atop the ground and secure its ends against flapping in the wind by placing the crates on them.

Use your tools to set each torch vertical and each stake spike-bottom down, deep enough that a medium-hard shaking doesn't dislodge them. Remove and gather the flags or torch-setting markers.

Fill the container inserts two thirds full with fuel. Unscrew their wick lids, pour in the liquid, and then tightly recap them. Tie a dangling glow stick below each cup to snap if wind makes the flame blow dangerously horizontal or the torch fuel is depleted. Use long matches or a long-barreled butane lighter to kindle the torches. Revel in your wisdom of spurning soulless street fluorescents in favor of being encircled by moving torchlight.

TORCH SPELLS

MAGICAL TORCH DÉCOR

On a Friday during daylight, decorate a tiki to your liking or to reflect the theme of an upcoming outdoor circle, gathering, or Sabbat. Scissor a silk flower lei into four quarters. Tie a knot in all the ends to prevent the flowers from falling off and then tie one each onto four tiki stakes, below the cup. Or you can do one of the following: embellish the tiki wood with glow-in-the-dark paint or the cup slats in strokes of Quarter colors; twine star-spangled garland wire or a string of gemstones around the stake; snake silk ribbons, Mardi Gras beads, strands of faux pearls, or pendant necklaces through the gaps in the woven fuel-canister housing cup; or replace the flimsy plastic snuffer string with a hemp braid and fetishes made of silver metallic arts-and-crafts clay that you harden with oven heat.

ALTERNATIVES: Camouflage your torches to blend in with the outdoor environment: Spatter them with paint that mirrors the colors of the seasons in which you plan to use them adoors:

Winter—black, gray, and beige

Spring/summer—light green, dark green, and gray

Autumn—brown, rust, and gray-orange

COME-HITHER CHANT

Torches naturally resemble the penis and the Witch's priapic[128] fertility wand composed of a fennel stalk with a pinecone or spiky dried sycamore pod atop it: The torch's handle equates with the stalk, and the bulgy fiber or combustible plant material above it with the head of the generative male organ. The heat that a torch emits is similar to the female body temperature that promotes fetal gestation.

Heighten sexual tension, goad greenwooding, and encourage conception by casting sacred space and holding a torch aloft in your left hand.

Chant this Greek quatrain while skipping sunwise:

> "MOONLIGHT FILÍ, TO PÁTHOS EVDAIMONÍA. I AGÁPI
> DEÍCHNOUN, EFCHARÍSTISI GNORÍZOUN."
> ["Moonlight kiss, passion bliss. Love show, pleasure know."]

---

128 Priapus is the olde Greek God depicted as a penis with feet or a male with a gigantic erect member.

FIRE MAGIC: MASTERING THE ELEMENT

"The most powerful weapon on earth is the human soul on fire."

—Ferdinand Foch, Key commander, latter days of World War I

CAMPFIRE AND BALEFIRE SPELLS

You'd think it would go without saying, but there's a goodly way to light a fire and an ungoodly way that's doomed to failure. This is the case because many people aren't trained from childhood to differentiate wet wood from dry "deadfall" wood that naturally falls on the ground because of age, blight, seasonal weather damage or tree lifespan. Nor do many people know the most efficient way to lay a fire, what makes the best fire-starter tinder, how to light a charcoal to burn incense atop, or how to scry a fire and foretell the future, among many fire Mysteries.

Properly dried wood is that from which you can remove bark flakes by using your fingernail. Glean the entire area around your site. Collect wee fragile splinters from inside fallen logs and then twigs, branches, limbs, and logs in varying levels of thickness and length.

If you're camping in fine conditions and want to thrill to a bewitching night fire, gather more wood than you think you could possibly need during midday. Not only is it goodly camper etiquette to leave some to benefit the next campers who come along, but truth is, Witches are fire-greedy, so you'll often find that you need twice as much wood as you thought before you get your fill of fire.

Near the fire pit you've dug and encircled with stones, stack the wood into separate piles according to size. If the wood is properly dry, you can snap all but thick limbs and logs to make it fit inside your fire pit by holding each end horizontally over your shin and pulling the ends toward you. If you must cut some logs to fit the pit, use a handsaw because a noisy, battery-operated, or belching gasoline-powered chain saw shatters the peace of natural wildlife habitats.

If fog, mist, or rain clouds approach, cover the wood with a plastic tarp and tuck it in to minimize dampness or stack it inside a tent and hope that it dries out before you need it.

Protect your Covenmates from getting hypothermia if everyone's camping adoors and vicious cold wet weather moves in and thwarts the burning of a warming fire: Sleep as a group beneath your heavy wool capes. If you have alcohol on hand, pass the frigid time in Pagan fashion by passing the bottle around while telling tall tales, topping one another's magical exploits, sharing ancient myth stories, chanting, singing, fortune-telling, and whatnot.

Reserve from your wood stash one tallish, stafflike stick to use as a fire poker: Witches' magical staves are leaned against trees, so lean it prominently against one to try to prevent it from being accidentally burned as your wood stock diminishes. Then sit and strip each twig, branch, and limb of any dry leaves or needles that can rise with fire heat, combust like flash paper, waft crackling high above, and catch arching tree canopies alight.

Next, tweak your tinder—thin, papery wood that serves as the base bed for all the firewood. The best is decaying pith beneath bark or from hollow logs. Discard any wet pieces and keep only the dry flakes.

Hand dig out a small hollow in the center of your fire pit and put several palms' worth of tinder in it. Avoid using lighter fluid or gasoline: Instead, put a match to a small "fire-brand" twig and use it to set the tinder alight.

Carefully shelter the infant flame you have produced from being blown out by the wind. When it seems strong enough to tolerate the wind without being smothered, add atop it successively larger twigs and saplings until it is roaring strongly enough to catch your first big log aflame.

Continue feeding and blowing your fire to life as it seems to require, always cognizant of the prevailing weather conditions, the time of day or night, whether you want to use it to cook, and when you plan to crash in your tent or shelter. Occasionally use your pokey stick to shift the wood around so that unlit sides are flipped atop the glowing coals and burn evenly and efficiently.

Don't make the trees' sacrifice be in vain: Use the fire's power for warmth or to bond with Covenmates. Toss dried herbs in bulk in the campfire to infuse your realm with instant enchantment and divine the future by interpreting the crackle and sizzle of the fire.

Stare intently into the fire or coals to see images of future events, warnings from the Goddess, or Fire Elemental salamanders dancing amid the flames. While scrying, listen for the sounds of nature: circling wildcats, hooting owls, croaking frogs, screech owls, and things that go bump in the night. Feel the presence of the ghosts and spirits of travelers from days gone by.

Tell a myth or debate principles of craft cosmology, Pagan philosophy, or quantum physics.

Share liquid spirits—traditionally the easiest way to attract Will-o'-the-Wisps. You may see the neon fairies amid the tree line or boldly floating single file in an air parade through the center of your campsite!

CAULDRON COOKING

IF YOU WANT TO COOK ADOORS:

Vertically set two strong bifurcated branches (shaped like the letter "Y") into the ground opposite each other beyond the fire pit's rock lining boundary. Sharpen one end of a straight stick to serve as a meat spit that campers can revolve by hand. Place it horizontally across the fire pit so that the bases of the branches' bifurcation support it. Or you can bring a flat metal oven rack from home, balance it atop the fire pit's stones, and heat or boil food in small to medium-size cooking pots on it.

If you'd prefer to cook in an iron cauldron that has hanging chains, use a heavy L-shaped branch to support it. Set the long straight part into the ground beyond the fire pit's rock lining and attach the chains to the short horizontal section pointing over the fire. If your cauldron lacks chains, set it directly onto the fire's coals and monitor it to prevent the contents from boiling over and dousing the fire.

Avoid burning chemically treated wood, which will off-gas noxious fumes. Never pitch plastic, metal, or glass into a fire, for the smoke that plastic and metal produce can be toxic and glass can shatter and explode out of a fire pit, ruining the site for future campers.

When it's time for sleep, "bank" your fire by tossing atop the coals the ashes that it has made; this often keeps a few coals smoldering overnight to make relighting easy the next morning. Just ensure that there's no way a stray spark could possibly set your tent or shelter alight and check on this when you rise to relieve yourself in the wee hours of the night.

To master cauldron, camping, and open-hearth cooking, read any of the following illustrated how-to books:

Dressing & Cooking Wild Game: From Field to Table—Big Game, Small Game, Upland Birds & Waterfowl, Teresa Marrone (Creative Publishing International, 1987.) Includes recipes and illustrated color how-to photos *Food in England*, Dorothy Hartley, Little, Brown, originally published in 1954, reprinted in 2006. Excellent pen-and-ink illustrated tips for outdoor cooking.

Simply Savory: Magical & Medieval Recipes, Lady Passion (2010). With hand-tinted olde woodblock illustrations. Includes a complete meal cooked in a cauldron and traditionally based menus for the eight annual Wiccan Sabbats.

The *Foxfire* series, Eliot "Wig" Wigginton (Anchor Books).

The Magic of Fire: Hearth Cooking—One Hundred Recipes for the Fireplace or Campfire, William Rubel (2004).

CREATURE MUSIC SPELL

If you're camping sufficiently far away from human population, say, 15 or more miles from civilization, animals and birds may join in your magical chanting or extemporaneous music playing around the campfire.

One year when my Coven and I were camping way out in the wilds of Appalachia, we became so inspired by our entrancing campfire that we instinctively grabbed for anything natural that we could bang together to celebrate the moment. Some tapped river stones together, some drummed sticks atop logs, others rattled pebbles in empty plastic water bottles. Each Witch built upon a primal rhythm—some keeping the beat while others played off the harmony. We played softly but steadily, and the fauna soon chimed in appreciatively: Tree frogs, cicadas, crickets, mating screech owls, even mountain lions! The wild cats paced around our tent compound adding their own low mew to the mix but we feared not—their paw-falls connoted happiness, not aggression. It was a very touching, unforgettable magical experience.

Make soft sounds with your feet or fingers, or bring or gather on-site natural items that can emit a sound when whacked together, tapped on, or rattled, such as the following:

Tapping barefoot on the ground—sounds like heartbeats.

Finger snapping—mimics cricket song.

Hand-sized flat river stones—sound like metallic marimbas when you strike one on another.

Two wet-wood sticks—have a muffled, banged drumming sticks sound when struck together.

A wet-wood stick and a log—can produce multiple tones depending on the log's degree of decay and where you hit it with the stick.

Tiny pebbles and an aspirin bottle—Witches often pack aspirin to treat hangovers: Sure an' we love to carry on carefree, we just don't relish suffering for it. Temporarily remove the pills and replace them with pebbles. Sounds like a rattle filled with rice.

Plant pods and a paper bag—Place the pods in the bag, blow air into it, then tie off the top and shake. Sounds like a shell-webbed gourd rattle.

If you light a campfire while camping at spring's end, make music while singing the circa 1240 Medieval English song "Sumer Is Icumen In." The round or, *rota* madrigal can be sung by up to six people, indicative of the ancient Pagan six-pointed symbol of the Sun called by Jews "the Star of David." It is an anonymously attributed song purportedly writ in Middle Age Southern English (Berkshire or Wiltshire) dialect. The British Museum houses the 1240 manuscript of the lyrics[129] that once resided with monks in Reading Abbey.

Also called "the cuckoo song" for the lyrics' mimicry of the bird yarble at the end, "Sumer" has the distinction of being the earliest Canon known. The songs words are decidedly Pagan and popularized by Paul Giovanni for the cult classic movie *The Wickerman* starring the late actor Christopher Lee. The following is the song's lyrics with a translation into present-day English:

> Sumer is icumen in, *(Summer has come in,)*
> lhude sing cuccu! *(loudly sing, Cuckoo!)*
> Groweth, sed and bloweth med *(Seed grows and meadow blooms)*
> and springth e wde nu, *(and springs the wood anew,)*
> Sing cuccu! *(Sing, Cuckoo!)*
> Awe bleteth after lomb, *(Ewe bleats after the lamb,)*
> lhouth, after calve cu. *(cow lows after the calf.)*
> bulluc sterteth, bucke verteth, *(bullock stirs, stag starts,)*

---

129 In folio 11v of Harley manuscript 978, British Museum's Digitized Manuscripts site.

murie sing cuccu! (merrily sing, Cuckoo!)
Cuccu! Cuccu! (Cuckoo! Cuckoo!)
Wel singes u cuccu— (Well sings the Cuckoo—)
ne swik thu naver nu." (Don't ever stop now.)
Round chorus interspersed at will:
"Sing cuccu, nu, (Sing cuckoo, now.)
Sing, cuccu." (Sing, Cuckoo.)

If you burn a fire while camping during the Lammas Sabbat (which Witches also call "the first harvest" play and sing the 1999 lyrics of "The Harvest" by Lisa Theriot of Raven Boy Music. This Pagani song links the human cycle of life and rebirth with the death-sacrifice reaping of John Barleycorn in His prime in order to nourish folk with food and liquor, and advises people to keep their own inevitable demise in mind, but also to take heart in their equally inevitable reincarnation.

"They tell the tale at Harvest time
of a man they call John Barleycorn—
a young man cut down in his prime
so that his soul might be reborn.
His seed is put into the ground,
and as the season turns around,
he rises up to meet the sky
only to be cut down by the Harvest.
Chorus: Round the seasons come and go . . .
high and mighty are laid low.
hand the reaper what you sow,
for you will climb,
but then it's time to be ready for the Harvest.
John Barleycorn will pay the price
our daily bread and grain to yield—
cut down as a sacrifice
like youth upon a battlefield—
What a gift he has to give,
that he should die that we might live,

Man can know no greater love,
and we enjoy the blessings of the harvest.
Chorus: Round the seasons come and go . . .
high and mighty are laid low.
hand the reaper what you sow,
for you will climb,
but then it's time to be ready for the Harvest.
And in the gather do you feel . . .
one more turning of the wheel?
Remember when you sow the seed
the neck that feels the reaper's blade—
and so your life becomes, indeed
the corners turned, and choices made.
Remember when you seek the light,
to every morning comes the night,
and when you feast and have your fill
don't forget it's only till the Harvest.
Chorus: Round the seasons come and go . . .
high and mighty are laid low.
hand the reaper what you sow,
for you will climb,
but then it's time to be ready for the Harvest.

If you burn a fire while camping during the Mabon Sabbat (which Witches also call "the second harvest"), play and sing "Scarborough Fair." This Dorian mode canticle ballad is oft sung as a duet. It involves the English town Yorkshire and its popular medieval gathering full of rare wares and roaming entertainers. While its lyrics were first found in 1673 bound at the end of a copy of Blind Harry's book *Wallace* printed in Edinburg, Scotland, the song is likely of earlier origin; similar words appear in the circa 1650 song "The Elfin Knight." Regardless of its age, it takes its rightful place along with many other poems and songs that entail devil dares posed humans, rhyming riddle songs, and those in which couples demand impossible tasks of each other as signs of their loyalty.

Scarborough Fair began every August 15th and lasted 45 days—ah, the days of arcady are gone, and over is their antique joy. Wouldn't we all love to celebrate in like fashion as folk did for centuries until such fairs were outlawed?

The Goodly Spellbook explains that the tag-line lyrics "parsley, sage, rosemary, and thyme" comprise an olde herbal contraceptive recipe of interest to Pagans who like to go "green-wooding" (a Witch word meaning making love adoors during warm seasons).[130]

If you camp or build a bonfire at Samhain, play instruments while singing the olde "Lyke-Wake Dirge." Writ in old Northern Yorkshire English dialect, this song encourages people to act ethically throughout life by helping the needy, and warns of repercussions at death if you ignore poverty and despair.[131]

To these Pagani song examples you can add myriad seasonal others, and experiment enthusiastically with producing specific rhythms whose magical effects on people are explained and illustrated in *The Goodly Spellbook*. Practice makes perfect: Use diverse ways of making sound, such as stomping, tapping, clapping, humming vowels and consonants, and make and play instruments composed of natural components, such as shaking a West African *shekere* (a dried gourd web-strung with beads) or shaking an empty container rattle filled with gemstone chips.

CAMPFIRE COCKTAIL CURE

Being immersed in nature is innately relaxing, but the next morning you may feel an *afterclap* [132] from backpacking, hiking, lifting firewood logs, stooping to erect a tent, and cavorting in front of a fire. For example, true tales are told of me unzipping my tent, only extending my hand, making a "bring me" motion with it, and plaintively mewing, "By the Great Horned Spoon, aspirin and coffee, *please*!"

PREPARE AHEAD OF TIME: Use a banked fire's radiant heat to steep a soothing toddy overnight for any to imbibe the next day as the effects of roughing it may necessitate.

BRING FROM HOME: A clean empty Mason jar with its rubber sealed lid. Add any or a combination of the following ingredients to a bit of clear liquor. Strain off plant matter and sip the liquid until you feel relieved.

Freshly harvested or dried peppermint spice or marshmallow root

> (settles the tummy).

---

130 Non-Witches contend that the romantic meaning of flower species is operative here. During the Victorian era, parsley equated with ease, sage meant longevity, rosemary represented love, and thyme connoted courage.
131 Innumerable print and local versions online. Reclaiming Collective word change from "May Christ" to "May Earth receive thy soul." Ae means "one"; hosen means "stockings"; shoon means "shoes"; whinnes means "thorns"; bane means "bone"; brid means "bridge"; nana means "none"; sal means "shall"; and saule means "soul."
132 A Witch word meaning "an action's unintended effects or undesired consequences."

Dried willow-bark or powdered aspirin (eliminates headache).

True Lime™ (small foil packets of crystals rich in vitamin C to forefend sniffles or illness after exertion).

Dried tea (energizes, reduces appetite, and is replete with antioxidants).

Dried feverfew (eases breathing after smoke inhalation, reduces inflammation, breaks a fever, and relieves headache).

When you're ready to leave the forest for home, quench the fire by throwing on it some stream water or remaining drinking water that you packed to the site. Then use your fire-stirring pokey stick to vigorously stir the ashes to ensure that all the embers are thoroughly extinguished.

FIRE FESTIVALS

The following are some of *many* opportunities from cultures worldwide to participate in celebratory light and fire feasts, rites, and Sabbats:

* OCTOBER 8, 1871.

* SAMHAIN (HALLOWEEN), OCTOBER 31ST. Participants in this Pagan Sabbat honor their Ancestors, friends, and loved ones or folk they admired who Crossed Over to the Summerlands during the previous year. Samhain marks Witches' New Year.

* DIWALI (DEEPAVALI), VARIOUS DATES ON OR NEAR NOVEMBER 15TH. Participants in this Asian Indian fest honor the wealth Goddess Lakshmi. Attendees attract prosperity by lighting candles inside rice-paper lanterns and releasing them with a wish, in the air like balloons.

* YULE (WINTER SOLSTICE), DECEMBER 21ST OR 22ND. Participants in this Pagan Sabbat mark the rebirth of the Sun God and bedeck our homes and yards with boughs, candles, and sparkly things. We may re-enact the mock battle between the Oak King and the Holly King, burn a Yule log, and scry firelight until sunrise.

* IMBOLC (CANDLEMAS/GROUNDHOG DAY), FEBRUARY 1ST OR 2ND. Participants in this Pagan Sabbat celebrate "the lambing of the ewes" (pregnant female lambs giving birth), and defy the last of winter dearth by turning on all the lights in their Covenstead or home.

* WALPURGISNACHT (VAPPU), APRIL 30TH. Participants in this nighttime German-origin celebration honor the Pagani-Christian female saint named Walpurga, and spring's return by making merry, rioting in Berlin, or singing spring folk songs and dancing around balefires.

* BELTANE, MAY 1. Participants in this Pagan Sabbat celebrate spring's arrival by dancing around balefires and attract fertility by weaving ribbons onto a tall, flower-crowned phallic wooden Maypole.

* BIRTHDAYS. Participants celebrate the day they were born and another year lived by lighting and then working wish magic while blowing out one or more vertical candles set in icing atop a cake.

* LITHA (SUMMER SOLSTICE), JUNE 21ST OR 22ND. Participants in this Pagan Sabbat celebrate the Sun's zenith most powerful aspect in the sky above, and may dance around a balefire, leap a cauldron fire, or reenact a twice-a-year mock battle between the Oak King and the Holly King (the Oak King is cut down in his prime as the Pagani song "The Harvest" describes. The Holly King reigns until the battle is repeated at Yule, when the tables are turned and the Oak King wins—counter-intuitive, I know, what with the association of Yule with boughs of holly and all, but there you have it.

* PAGAN FIRE-FOCUSED GATHERINGS by various names that often include fiery theme title words such as "ignite" and "kinetic" in the fest's title. Held on diverse dates and at many locations worldwide.

* ALL SABBATS AND HOLY PAGAN TIMES can include a feast of foods in season and spirits that correspond to the time of year: sharp, refreshing stuff in spring and summer and warming toddies in fall and winter.

Of course, you don't have to reserve working fire magic only for traditional sacred times: Add verve to *any* festival, gathering, rite, or spell by decorating your Covenstead or home with candelabra or decorating adoors with tall tiki torches or lining a processional path with sand-weighted paper bag luminaries lit with an inset tea light or votive candes to light the way for folk to walk toward a cast circle destination.

Leap a cauldron fire, spin fire or LED-lit *poi*; toss pyrotechnics in a bale fire. Burn paper scrolls to waft a wish to the Gods' attention or to banish a bad habit or dispel ill luck. All these options and any creative ideas you may conceive should be designed to honor, appeal to, or appease a deity or Element.

Witches nurture fire's *feelings* because we believe that in a spiritual sense, every flame deserves to dance until satisfied. At gatherings we're the last ones to linger over the embers to see the fire's final flash. Only tree frogs, cicadas, and crickets witness our ardor.

However, to be truly fire proficient, you must know how to ice its temperament if need be. For instance, if it breaks out in your presence, part of what you might do to counter it is to whisper appropriate Barbarous Words of Power from *The Goodly Spellbook* while trying to douse, smother, or otherwise put it out. A goodly example is intoning the word *Omdour* to dispel argument or strife, and by extension, to extinguish fire or mute threatening lightning, etc. (Its reverse, *Roudmo,* causes discord).

PUBLIC FIRE RITUALS

If you work magic in public say, during a Sabbat, carefully consider your lighting options. Depending on where you live, the country or city may have lax or strict rules about what kind of open flame you can burn, when, and where.

Drought and dry weather streaks can preclude your ability to burn a Witchy bonfire. Wind conditions, ritual proximity close to a fire hydrant, city ordinances, the time your rite is scheduled—all these factors can be mitigating circumstances that will dictate what, if any, additional lighting you may choose to use.

There are times when circling beneath pure moonlight is best, times when tall, sickly orange city lights should be countered by employing a distracting color or kind of light alternative, and times when nothing less than a raging fire will suffice.

Observe ahead of time every lighting permutation of your planned or reserved/permitted circling space or ritual site. Note how it appears at morning daybreak, in noonday sun, during twilight fade, and in dim moon-glow so that you can create ways to maximize pretty reflections, entrance participants, or distract them from odious light that could impede their magical focus.

Be light adaptable. For example, over more than two decades I've used all manner of creativity to light my public night rites. Examples that really seemed to touch folk were during a French Broad River forest park rite in which hundreds danced to traditional gypsy music while spinning neon blue glow sticks; and another public Samhain rite when my Covenmates and I wrapped a mile or so of pentagram foil garland onto tall, soil-inset sticks to create a labyrinth over acres, in which all danced and processed, and that reflected tiki torchlight and moonlight to enable folk to easily navigate its convolutions.

As above, so below: As with lighting a Coven camping fire, you'd think it would go without saying, but in fact, there's a right way and a wrong way to construct an impressive fire meant to inspire hundreds attending a Pagan gathering or participating in a Sabbat. But when folks aren't taught from an early age to be proficient in making a fire to warm themselves, they are unlikely to be savvy about how to create big fires to warm and entertain a horde.

Modern bonfires[133] differ from Witchcraft balefires in several respects. For one thing, these days bonfires are rarely sacred in nature; indeed, most are used to celebrate a sports victory or to burn books, a flag, or a reviled figure in effigy, such as a dictator, suspected traitor, or perceived enemy such as a Witch. Most gruesomely, they're often made by crooks to try to eliminate evidence of their crimes, and they're often composed of hazardous materials piled high to induce emotional frenzy of participants.

In contrast, the word "balefire" refers to bound faggots[134] or natural combustibles used to fuel a blaze, such as a bale of dry grass. As such packaging implies, time and care are taken to make this kind of Witch fire last. Compacting the materials ekes out every possible flame so that it witnesses the sunrise or the last holdout drummer to reluctantly shuffle off to bed.

Balefires are made intentionally pure to encourage people to dance for hours around them or to leap them when they die down. They never include varnished furniture wood or anything similar that would set off allergies or inhalation pneumonia in those enjoying their blaze.

---

133 Bon, French, meaning "good."
134 An olde word for the bound piles of dry limbs used to burn heretics and Witches.

There are taboos associated with balefires, based on common sense. No one has to be told not to toss tobacco butts, plastic, or trash in a balefire, or not to light it before the main rite: It's understood that one or more folks are in charge of setting it up, lighting it, stoking it, and extinguishing it.

Frequently, those in charge of hosting a gathering or officiating at a Sabbat are too busy dealing with other details to tend to the fire as well, so they delegate the building and maintenance of it to young, strong, exuberant males who often appear to believe that their mere presence is enough to spark and vouchsafe the fire.

Au contraire: Too oft these spend all day chain-sawing gigantic pieces of wood to size with such noisy fanfare that it aggravates hangovers and annoys wildlife. Then they pile it in tipi fashion as high as their hubris: As the wood burns, the logs fall in on themselves and can roll or crash in ways that defy anticipation, with their efforts imperiling the crowd just when they're full of magical merriment. If folks are told to line up in single file, approach, and put something *into* the fire, some among the number could easily be burned.

Some may even try to sneak in inappropriate chemical lighting solutions to explode the balefire, which then burns too hotly and quickly. This can be propane, lighter fluid, or a combustible mixture that they devise and are the only ones who know its complete composition.

Although there's often an element of danger in working magic, shortcuts taken while making a ritual focal fire could conceivably cost lives. So as with a campfire, start a big balefire small and steadily build it until it is stable enough to have hundreds circle it safely. Extinguish it with water as you would a campfire.

After the main rite, Pagans often dance, talk, play musical instruments, and drink and flirt around the balefire until dawn. It's fine if you want to squirt spirits from a bota bag[135] into the mouths of balefire dancers you admire, but if you do, protect them from becoming so entranced by the flames that they walk or stumble into them—a more common happening than you'd think!

In addition, many Witches scry balefires with such unblinking intensity that they awake the next morn with their eyes swollen shut from heat desiccation. Prevent this by passing around a squirt bottle with pre-made soothing eyewash water in it that is made of steeped and strained feverfew, eyebright, and rose petals.

---

135 Traditional Spanish wineskin container typically made of goatskin or leather.

ANCIENT HILL FIRE-WHEEL ROLLING

Considered an improvement on a sixth-century French method of publicly executing people by forcing them into a ditch and driving over them in a laden wagon, the bone-breaking wheel was a torture device used postmortem in Prussia/Germany as late as 1841.[136]

An accused person was lashed facedown atop a wagon wheel, sometimes with spikes driven into it, or roasted from the front (underneath) while being tortured on their back to force them to confess.

---

136 Matthias Blazek, *Letzte Hinrichtung durch Rädern im Königreich Preußen am 13.* (In Prussia a criminal was broken upon the wheel on August 13, 1841.)

Convicts were tied onto the wheel and dragged behind a wagon to their place of execution. There they were either rolled down a rocky hill and left for carrion food or beaten with a club or cudgel "top down" (neck first, immediately fatal) or "bottom up," with their spines snapped and their limbs broken above and below their elbows and kneecaps,[137] their crushed appendages then woven between the wheel's spokes, their head nailed onto the wheel,[138] and their wounded body lashed up high on a tall pole to prevent rescue, induce sunburn, and attract scavenger birds that pecked at their mangled parts.

Some survived for days in pitiable agony until they succumbed to blood loss, dehydration, exposure, or shock. Afterward, their remains were set ablaze, rolled downhill, and left to rot, or their heads were cut off and displayed on a spike.

Nor was Europe an aberration: North America used the wheel after a 1712 slave uprising, and 11 were killed with it in Louisiana between 1730 and 1754.

I don't relate this gory litany gratuitously but rather to illustrate that this was a depraved degeneration of Pagan "wheel" rolling rites intended to *celebrate* life during the summer solstice.

Re-enact the goodly olde way of working wheel magic for the main ritual at sunset during the Lesser Sabbat Litha (midsummer). Gather the celebrants atop a hill with a long smooth slope. Ensure that no one is on the slope, and have water, sand, or extinguishers close by.

Light candles and incense, cast circle, and chant, sing, and make merry. When anticipation is high, thrust a sapling 2 to 3 inches (5.08 to 7.62cm) wide through the flat center of a large rolled bale of hay so that it extends on each side about the width of three pairs of hands. Mechanically, the limb will act as a stabilizing axle and push bars for up to three people per side; magically, thrusting a straight piece into a round one mimics sex and confers fertility, virility, and vitality.[139]

Depending on your bale's heft, have two, four, or six folks don insulated gloves as you torch the hay ablaze. Have them grip the wood protrusions and gently push the bale off the summit: Gravity will take the round down the hill. The rolling, burning bale *really* resembles the Sun and leaves a blazing trail like a fire dragon.

---

137 The fifteenth-century blood court in Zurich is an example of the legal prescription of the number and placement of blows.

138 This head nailing is the origin of the English expression "I've racked my brains, but I just can't remember . . ."

139 We also do this when we penetrate a cup of wine with an athamé blade to bless an offering to the Gods during the Cakes & Wine ceremony after spellwork.

Divine how the community will fare by interpreting how easy or difficult the bale was to light, how smoothly or wobbly it rolled, whether it rolled straight or veered, and how fast or weakly it burned.

Use the remainder at the bottom of the hill as a base for a balefire. Dance around it to mimic the spheres of the hay and Sun.

See a video of German farmers conducting this rite in 2015: https://www.youtube.com/watch?v=Q7ohJ1Si8yE.

ALTERNATIVE: Climax the festivities with fireworks as the German farmers did.

BRAVE FIRE WALK

This rite is not for the faint of heart or those lacking courage. It *is* doable for the average Pagan of goodly heart.

Pagan cultures worldwide have conducted and perpetuated fire walking for eons. The practice's earliest reference was in a story that dates back to India in the Iron Age, circa 1,200 B.C.E.

We do it for diverse reasons, such as to show religious devotion; as a rite of passage to display bravery or maturity; as a challenge while Initiating someone into the Mysteries; to forefend summer drought and wildfire; to mark a fire Sabbat; or to invigorate depleted cropland. Counter-intuitively perhaps, some countries hold the ritual during the longest, hottest day of the year at the summer solstice, when the Sun is at His zenith.

Not all walks feature wood; some substitute smooth stones heated in a fire. Some lay down a bed of coals directly atop the ground, others surround the embers with low wooden containment beams to prevent coal rolling, and still others opt to play it safe by hiring a company that specializes in setting up walks for corporate employee retreats or self-improvement seminars.

Burns and blisters seem most typically caused when someone doesn't walk fast enough with flat feet and when the coals or stones are improperly prepared.

If you would try this spiritual exercise, follow the commonsense rules and be vigilant and safety-conscious. Do the following:

* Clean the site of hazards such as glass shards and metal flotsam.

* In the same vein, never burn wet or green wood, only well-dehydrated hardwood. Some intersperse untreated charcoal throughout the walk path because it insulates against heat four times better than hardwood does; you'd obviously want to

avoid burning charcoal impregnated with chemicals to make it burn hot, because it would emit toxic fumes and increase the likelihood of blisters and burns.

* Further reduce singeing of soles by evaporating as much internal water as the wood or coals may yet retain, by burning them and then letting them cool and further desiccate in the ambient air.

* As the wood makes coals and embers, use shovels to bank the ashes to the sides of the walkway. This will enable you to sprinkle a thin layer of ash atop the embers when they're ready for folk to walk on—when they glow but produce no major new heat.

* Lay a water-drenched rug or soaked carpet remnant at the walk's end to soothe feet or help remove any coal bits that may cling to the feet.

* Let coal spreaders rest before attempting to cross: Indeed, *all* who participate should be rested—and sober enough not to already be walking sideways.

* Station a facilitator at the beginning of the straightaway to prevent runners from carrying anything, such as a cup of wine or a stabilizing wooden staff, and to prevent them from attempting the walk while wearing a cape, robe, or gossamer garb. The facilitator should insist that everyone minimize burn risk by going skyclad (a Witch word meaning naked).

* Stagger additional enablers near the sides of the route and at the end of the hot row. Task them to prevent embers from tumbling toward spectators; prevent stumbling, panic, and burns; and to enthusiastically congratulate all who succeed.

* Many people claim that having dry feet can reduce scalding, so you may want to provide a towel to enable this.[140] Others insist that wet feet are a bit protective, so you may want to supply a water bucket if you want to try this tack. Still others contend that those who frequently walk around barefoot or cultivate calluses on their soles will fare better than tenderfeet will.

* Reduce fear and increase nerve by having folk line up to take their turn far enough away from the stones or embers that they don't intensely feel their radiance.

---

140 It would be interesting if someone studied and compiled data regarding whether "wet Sun sign types" such as Pisces fare better at fire walks than "dry astrological signs" such as Leo.

* The facilitator should remind folk of the core basics before they begin: Walk briskly but don't run, as this can cause pockets of hot air to form and disturb the embers, increasing the potential to scald or burn the top of the feet. Avoid curling or splaying toes and raising the arch of the foot above the coals, as this encourages radiant heat that can blister.

* Foster a supportive group bond and synchronize heartbeats by having some folk play a steady drum rhythm or sing this quatrain:

> *"I love the fire.*
> *It wills us to be free.*
> *I love the fire.*
> *And the fire loves me."*[141]

An impressive number of Pagans are professional health-care providers (nurses, physical therapists, masseuses, etc.), so have a few of these roam about and assess and treat fire walkers who may be in such ritual bliss that they're unaware of singes or blisters.

Soothing herb-based skin balms, spray aloe vera with lidocaine, wet cotton foot wraps, and a swig or two from a drinking horn afterward work wonders and can minimize morning-after regret.

FIRE SPELLS

Much has been made of Witches' penchant for burning parchment spells. Doing so quickly wafts our wants directly to the Gods' attention. Although there are times when nothing less will suffice, I feel strongly that of late such has become the go-to of lazy ilk, so don't be a one-trick pony by working this kind of fire magic to the exclusion of all others.

Balefires done rightly are deeply affecting, liberating, transformational, and even life changing. But Pagans can do more with fire than simply enjoy flames' dynamic dance.

TO ENJOY GREAT DAYS

Avoid unpleasantness and attract luck and ease by performing a morning spell popular with Asian Indians.

---

141 Lyrics by Lady Passion. The full song details Witch powers associated with all the four Elements.

Upon waking, look at your hands and intone the following magic charm:

"In the tips of the fingers resides Goddess Lakshmi.
In the middle, Goddess Saraswathi.
In the palm of the hand resides Goddess Parvati.
Looking at my hands, I begin my day."

TO HAVE LOVE RECIPROCATED

The following spell to Aphrodite is adapted from *PGM* IV.1265–74, which explicitly promises that your desire will be reciprocated if you perform it "in this way it will succeed."

Nepherie'ri is a description of the love Goddess Aphrodite meaning "the beautiful eye" (in modern parlance, bright eyes). Pronounce it Nehfir-*ihree*.

STAY PURE FOR THREE DAYS. ON THE THIRD NIGHT, BEGIN HONORING THE GODDESS APHRODITE WITH A NIGHTLY BURNT OFFERING OF FRANKINCENSE RESIN FOR A WEEK, EACH TIME INTONING O'ER THE SMOKE HER EPITHET NEPHERIE'RI. THEN APPROACH YOUR LOVE INTEREST WHEN YOU CAN OR WILL, GAZE INTENTLY AT THAT PERSON, AND THINK THE NAME SEVEN TIMES IN SUCCESSION.

TO STOP TEARS

Intentionally spill salt, pick it up, and throw it in a fire.

TO KNOW YOUR FATE

To discern your future, cut a few strands of your hair and set them alight: If they burn brightly, you will live long; hair that splutters or smolders portends death.

TO CONJURE CASH

Burn dried onion skins. Better yet, before you do, use a green ink marker to draw atop one the magic number square of Jupiter illustrated in *The Goodly Spellbook*.

ALTERNATIVE: Burn eggshells. Keep money *flowing in* by tossing eggshells in a fireplace so that they burn when you light a hearth fire.

LEO LEG CURE

This "talisman for the foot of the gouty man" from *The Demotic Magical Papyrus*, Verso Col. X,[142] can aid anyone who has a pedal injury or who suffers from diabetic neuropathy, a circulation disorder such as Reynaud's, plantar warts, bunions, or peripheral vascular disease.

ON A FRIDAY AT SUNRISE DURING A WAXING OR FULL MOON, FACE THE WEST DIRECTION AND BURN A BLUE CANDLE AND CAMPHOR INCENSE. YOU WRITE THESE NAMES ON A STRIP OF SILVER OR TIN;[143] YOU PUT IT ON A DEER-SKIN,[144] YOU BIND IT TO THE FOOT OF THE MAN . . . THEN INTONE "THEMBARATHEM OUREMBRENOUTIPE AIOKHTHOU SEMMARATHEMMOU (LO) NAIOOU. LET N.[145], SON OF N., RECOVER FROM EVERY PAIN WHICH IS IN HIS FEET AND TWO LEGS. YOU DO IT WHEN THE MOON IS IN THE CONSTELLATION OF LEO."[146]

ALTERNATIVE: Pisces rules the feet, so you could *also* work the spell during March.

TO PREVENT HOUSE FIRE

Do as those who live in Cornwall, England: Harvest, dry, and put seaweed in wooden frames. Place the frames atop your fireplace mantel. By the rules of magical correspondences as explained in *The Goodly Spellbook*, wet plants from the sea reduce fire risk.

TO PREVENT FIRE ANTS

The Japanese believe that ants are stingy, so post a written warning to them in your home, threatening to levy a cash tax on them if they dare try to take up residence.

SPARKLER RITUALS

Add sizzle to any outdoor spell or rite by chanting, singing, or dancing while holding lit fireworks sparklers whose color magically corresponds to your spell intention, as enacted by actress Ellen Burstyn in the movie *The Divine Secrets of the Ya-Ya Sisterhood*.

---

142 Bracketed material mine.
143 You could use inexpensive, ubiquitous tinfoil.
144 Despite their legs' visual delicacy, deer are strong, fleet runners.
145 "N" means fill in a magical target's name here in ancient grimoires such as the *PGM*.
146 The power of the fixed fire zodiac sign Leo can strengthen weak body parts.

Fire craft should not be reserved solely for adults. It can be incredibly inspiring to young people who deeply crave and *deserve* to be exposed to magic as a balm and antidote against the pressures of materialism, propaganda, and conformity.

Death is no respecter of persons or age, and so it was for my daughter when she was barely a teen. At the dawn of cyber-bullying—before it was a thing, had a name, or was roundly reviled—a girlfriend of hers apparently experienced it and committed suicide in grisly fashion at the tender age of 15.

We went to pay our respects at a local funeral home, where I was immediately surrounded by a group of bereft female classmates of hers who desperately whispered to me that they were horrified at the Christian rites her parents wanted because the deceased had converted to Paganism shortly before her demise.

They talked animatedly and rapidly, certain that she would be outraged at what was being done to her body and the way her family was painting the situation to others. They had obviously discussed the dilemma, because they already had a plan: They begged me to conduct a Rite for the Departed Soul for the girl and to let them participate. They had parental support, and so I agreed on the spot.

I went home and, having known the girl myself for years, devised a rite to honor her that would also be cathartic for her mourning friends.

I set the time for dusk. We all met up in a forestland home beside an Appalachian mountain river. The supportive parent and I imbibed a glass of wine, and I chatted with the crew and then set to work.

I wanted all of them to feel personally invested in the ritual's success, so I asked for their help in erecting an altar adoors. They led me to a lovely site where we wedged a large ornate mirror in a mighty oak's branches and set sparklers and tall yellow spiral wax tapers into the ground to demarcate the circle.

I didn't dismiss the gravity of the watershed moment in their lives by talking down to them: The hosting parent trusted me so implicitly that she didn't even bother to monitor.

I lit the tapers, cast solemn circle, then bade all of them to fully express their grief—to articulate their sadness, anger, frustration, confusion, and sense of vulnerability. Why did she do it? If *she* could, what chance did *they have of escaping the same fate?* Their reined-in tears flowed and wet their feet.

When all were spent, I changed the mood. I had them relate in adolescent detail the many happy moments that they had shared with their beloved dead, the talents of hers that they'd admired, and the unique mannerisms and funny foibles that she'd had. Each girl's eyes reflected the lesson imparted without preaching: Henceforth they would strive harder to appreciate the people around them.

I reassured them that hers had not been a one-shot life. I spoke gently about the rest and contentment that she was doubtlessly enjoying in the Summerlands. I assured them that she would reincarnate and would once again relish her love of magic. They listened intently as if no adult had ever told them the truth about anything in their lives.

The time of dark trees arrived—when bark turns black against the Sun's last setting sliver. They needed direction no more: I lit the sparklers as they twirled their bodies extemporaneously, relieved that their ritual had ensured that the girl would not turn into an angry ghost.

I passed the sparklers out, two per person.

I banished the circle with a flick of my wrist, and we all ran out carrying the lit champagne of fireworks that make people smile. We used them as air pens to express our final sentiments and well wishes to the girl.

All had stopped being weepy-distraught and feeling more than a little guilty for what they had or hadn't said and done. The survivors felt heard, heeded, and empowered. We bade the girl a final farewell and extinguished the sparklers in the river.

Ever remember that big Witches come from little Witches. People speak of letting kids be kids, but now more than ever, children truly need a magical education and magical encouragement in a raucous, arbitrary, difficult time. Like death, the lure of magic is no respecter of persons or age—it can attract anyone anytime.

HOT ROCKS DIVINATION

Invite folks to a stream-side ritual. Ask each to bring a shovel from home. Start a fire until it roars vigorously.

Have each person find a stone on-site to represent themself, think of a question or personal conundrum, and then put the stone in the shovel's metal "cup up" curve and hold the tool horizontally o'er the fire.

When the stones glow, bid all to quickly remove their implements from the fire and to lower them into the stream, careful not to let the water sweep their stone away.

Discuss the meanings of the omens that occur from the sounds that the stones emit when the water makes them sizzle, such as the following:

* CRACKLE—The Gods support your wish or idea. Go for it!

* CREAK—Your plan needs polishing to perfect.

* GROAN—The Gods have heard and answered this plea before.

* HISS—The Gods disapprove of your want, plan, or action.

* RIP—Your desire is doomed to fail. Ditch it immediately.

* SIZZLE—The Gods like where you're going with your idea.

* SQUEAK—Verbalize your dream: The squeaky wheel gets the grease!

* YAWP—Bereft isolation. Don't go forward with your plan.

* YIP—Like a quick, sharp wolf cub bark. Beware, danger afoot.

* YOWL—The Gods know you really want this. They'll aid you when your impulse or resolve fails.

Although these descriptions may sound subjective if you take them at face value, you will all enjoy debating the merits of arguments for or against this one or that one having occurred and quickly arrive at a consensus about what actually did happen and what it bodes.

MELTED METAL SPELL

Foretell events the olden way—by smelting lead. *Molybdomancy* is the Witch art of divining the future by interpreting the shape that molten metal forms when dripped into cold water.

INGREDIENTS:

Bowl	Cooking pot
Propane or Bunsen burner	Face mask
Cold water	Heat-resistant gloves

On a windy Saturday night, ponder a question. Don gloves and a mask and melt lead in a pot atop a burner. When the lead is liquefied, pour some into the bowl of cold water. Interpret the magic meaning of the symbolic shapes it forms as you would with candle wax *ceromancy*.

ALTERNATIVE: Melt fishing line weights.

LIGHTNING RITUAL

Zeus is the Greek equivalent of the Norse God Thor, Whose sacred symbol is the thunder hammer. Zeus's mythology maintains that He's randy and angry and defends against all comers, so Witches sometimes dare Him to manifest His signature omen lightning.

On a Thursday, preferably during a waxing or full moon, use traditional Witch ways to conjure sky fire. Dress in bluish white. Assemble spell components in your ritual space.[147] They could include a recording of hypnotic instrumental drumbeat music, cashew nuts, mirrors, or cardboard wrapped with aluminum foil, scissors, and whole dried chili peppers.

Witchy music to play. Sit cross-legged facing the South Elemental Fire direction. Light a red candle and, atop a lit coal, burn as incense one pepper at a time for as long as the spell requires.

Place shiny surfaces in front of you, but facing outward away from you. Hold shears in your right hand. Think about all the injustices that innocents suffer every second: Get outraged about its many manifestations and perverted permutations until you achieve an emotionally ballistic froth. As your anger threatens to explode, repeatedly open and close the shears aggressively.

Visualize yourself as Zeus's rival, desirous to prevent and eliminate injustice. Rise. Insist that He manifest. Taunt Him to appear as lightning by tossing the cashews in the air and stomping until He does.

Every aspect of the magical correspondences of the ingredients is designed to provoke Him, and should be self-evident except for the cashews and chili peppers, which represent penile erection. This is perhaps the most overt taunt of all to a God personified as without parallel in His sexual incorrigibility.

---

147 If adoors, don't perform beneath or hide under an oak because superstition insists that "it draws the stroke" (lightning).

DISPOSING OF FIRE REMAINS

It's goodly to recycle toxic components rather than expose the environment to them. Just avoid trying to *endlessly* recycle spell ingredients, for like humans, rite inclusions can grow weary of being overly relied upon, overused, or overworked. If you become a one-trick pony who only falls back on magic with which you're familiar, you may find that you cannot compel a component to mitigate on your behalf when you most need its might.

Here are some ways to dispose of fire spell ingredients:

* Some spell ingredients can be ingested; because they are edible, you can literally eat them to *eliminate* all traces. Examples include bread scored with a sacred fire symbol, spicey potions, and fruit and veggies carved with fire spell words writ in a magical alphabet.

* You can burn some fire spell stuff, such as wax, paper, and fabric.

* You can bury many spell ingredients and return them to Mother Earth from whence they derive.

* Biodegradable wick, metal, and spent ritual salt are examples. Depending on the type of spell you cast, you might bury the components in your own yard, on the spell target's property, or in a graveyard or waste place. Never make the act look obvious: None should be able to detect disturbed ground.

* If you don't want to risk slow breakdown by soil, you could use natural caustics such as borax and lye to speed the deterioration of rite remains.

* If the components are difficult to decipher, such as a leaf on which you wrote a magic square in lemon juice, you could expose it to the Elements by secreting it adoors.

* Some small spell ingredients can be flushed to the oblivion of the pipes by using a toilet's Coriolis force. Spent altar saltwater is a goodly example.

* You can offer some components adoors in a dish as a feast for animals or as offerings to fairies, God/desses, or Spirits. Examples include food and drink remains from the after spellwork Cakes & Wine ceremony, broken incense sticks, and broken bits of magical jewelry.

* As counterintuitive as it may seem, you can actually set some fire rite components on a current to be swept away by a river, stream, sea, or ocean. This is especially apt if you cast a spell to quell anger, argument, or strife.

* If you work a particularly complex fire spell, you may elect to dispose of its ingredients in diverse ways to prevent anyone from being able to figure out exactly what you did. For instance, you could eat some, flush some, burn, and bury some. I personally prefer this method as a rule.

CREMATION

Few like to consider this subject, but Witches don't shy away from the facts of life, and neither should you.

It is the nature of ash to waft where it will on the wind, to attach and settle on aught. Ash bonds with blades of grass, blends with flower pollen, and makes twigs look pregnant with raindrops. Ash melds with oceans of water molecules, rises to make magenta the sky, and descends to mineralize roots. Volcanic ash can kill only to later foster fertile fields. It is this cyclic philosophy that leads many a Witch to abhor the thought of experiencing a modern burial and embalming, which is scientifically impermanent.

First, the undertaker is often called to pick up the remains. Staff policy is to instantly form an exit plan to prevent being made to feel uncomfortable by family members' heartfelt expression of shock or grief. This is why they insist that a clear path be made to remove potential furniture impediments to the gurney and relegate relatives away while they transport the body.

Back at the biz, one or a pair clinically disembowel and eviscerate the remains. Some blood is drained and replaced with a chemical-water formalin solution.[148]

Embalming implements resemble medieval torture devices:

"AFTER YOU DIE, BLOOD POOLS IN YOUR ORGANS, AND ARTERIAL EMBALMING REMOVES ONLY A FRACTION OF YOUR BODY'S BLOOD. WE . . . REMOVE VARIOUS OTHER BODILY FLUIDS, AS WELL AS ANY URINE OR FECES THAT WASN'T EXPELLED WHEN YOU DIED (WHICH TOTALLY HAPPENS). TO DO THIS, WE USE A VACUUM-LIKE DEVICE CALLED AN ASPIRATOR THAT HAS AN ENORMOUS 20-INCH (50.8 CM) NEEDLE TOPPED WITH ONE OF THESE TIPS THAT TOTALLY AREN'T BASED OFF MEDIEVAL TORTURE DEVICES."[149]

---

148 Undertaker experts report that trying to massage the formalin into the tissues frequently causes postmortem erections in men. When time fails to resolve the dilemma, the penis is duct-taped to the leg to prevent detection.
149 Judge for yourself by viewing pictures of common embalming tools at thefuneralsource.org/faq.html.

The stuff that surrounds the guts is vacuumed or removed entire and oft replaced with cotton padding or whatnot. Sometimes a wig is stitched onto the skull. Bruises and such are covered with cosmetics, but gaping wounds are replaced with putty, wax, plaster of Paris, and unspecified "special materials" used to fake missing muscle and bone.

Undertakers report that the family pressure is extreme to make bodies look in any semblance as they did when alive regardless of whether the deceased was severely burned or even decapitated.[150] Some folk go so far as to request a "marionette funeral" in which the corpse's arms and legs are posed by strings.

The efforts to which they resort in order to make a body presentable haunt their memories and dreams. For example, dismembered body parts are oft separately prepared and basically slip stitched onto the torso on a super-temporary basis designed to last only through a brief viewing.

Being embalmed slows down decomposition for only a few weeks at the most and barely enables the scrutiny of cursory open-casket viewing. To Witches, it seems wrong to pay high dollars ourselves or to bankrupt our families for the privilege.

We consider other sobering truths as well regarding embalming dispensation of our electro-fiery remains, such as that cups that dig into eyelids are oft input to prevent the sunken-socket look. (Some undertakers use superglue or stitches to close the lids.) To keep the mouth closed and centered for viewing, techs use a needle injector to wire the gums and upper and lower jaw shut. The nose, rectum, and vagina are sometimes packed with cotton to temporarily prevent leaks into the casket.

Beyond all this macabre stuff, Pagans have a hard time believing that our demise should cause a tree to be felled for our coffin wood or that our bones should be confined in a steel vault. To us, all this is spit and baling wire to avoid inevitable decay and, put bluntly, revoltingly violent.

We know that embalming is a relatively modern phenomenon because in America before the Civil War at least, the practice had been largely used to preserve bodies for medical research. The surfeit of horrifically decomposed soldiers during hot railroad transport home at that time sparked a national hue and cry. Dr. Thomas Holmes marketed embalming as a scientific advancement—the costly alternative to plain burial that many folk now take for granted.

We know that few graveyards or mausoleums can be considered invulnerable to "progress": Many are eventually bulldozed to widen highways or to clear land

---

150 Heads are frequently re-attached by using a wood dowel.

for schools or are neglected next to busy, trashy grocery stores, as is one case in our Asheville town. I've witnessed all these insults and more in my own wee area of Appalachia.

We know that many graves are unmarked or lack a tombstone for a stretch of time, so bodies are not always properly located and are moved elsewhere. Even when they *are* properly located, they could well be interred in a pauper's field in a large city cemetery—not as originally envisioned by the deceased and the grieving family members who paid dearly to prevent such an atrocity.

We know that 1,400 and counting American funeral homes that appear to be locally operated are *actually* owned by the corporate conglomerate Service Corporation International (also known as Dignity Memorial® network).

We feel that it would be hubristic for us to take up excess space after death, to stake a posthumous claim on prime real estate—typically, rolling hills sporting some of the few large trees that aren't on the chopping block.

True, a few cemeteries in the United States now offer "natural burial"—wrapping the body in a fabric shroud and interring it simply in the ground. There's also a trend toward using compost and other natural materials to speed decomposition. But not everyone wants his or her body to be in proximity to other dead bodies.

Considering that Witches were burned at the stake for eons, it may seem ironic that some of us would prefer cremation, but it's understandable since many of us want to return to Mother Earth before reincarnating. Sure, our souls would reincarnate *regardless* of the death rite our bodies endured, but considering that dignity is difficult enough to preserve in life, we question why we would want to sacrifice it so willingly in death.

Some folks in Pagani countries such as India cling to the traditional practice of cremation despite a concerted governmental push to condemn and suppress it on the grounds that it poses a public health hazard or emits carbon monoxide and other gases into the environment.

Many wrongly believe that corpses spread disease by mere act of putrefaction, but this has been roundly denied by experts such as Steven Rottman,[151] who said on public record that cadavers pose *less* risk of contagion than living people. Some companies are even trying to divorce the process from the Element Fire altogether in favor of developing and promoting the supposed benefits of electric cremation.

---

151 Director, UCLA Center for Public Health and Disasters.

In the United States and many other countries "only crematories may cremate bodies. However, most crematories will allow for ceremonies *before* the cremation and will allow for guests to be present at the cremation itself."[152]

Cremation does not preclude a viewing, but this adds to the cost. Many Pagans prefer instead to hold a memorial service, a celebration of life ceremony, or a raucous three-day come-and-go-as-you-like wake or to bring the ashes into a sacred circle and honor the Beloved Dead in a traditional Rite for the Departed Soul.

Afterward, survivors oft disperse the ashes on land, sea, or in the adoors air as specified in a last Will & Testament, or as they feel that the person would have wanted. Some also wear a bit of the ashes of a loved one in jewelry. I have even seen some of a person's ashes shared in a smoking pipe at a Pagan gathering in the hope that a bit of the deceased's power would infuse the inhalers.

All people should choose their dispensation as they see fit, but a case has been made about the merits of cremation: It is simple, comparatively inexpensive, permanent, and more natural in many ways than a typical burial.

ASH SPELLS

Ritual ashes have been used in myriad ways since antiquity. For instance, after a fair or Sabbat, balefire ashes might be gathered and the lye by-product they produced used to whiten garments dirtied by attending the gathering.

SABBAT ASHES MAGIC

Store some ashes from every Sabbat balefire in their own lidded, labeled, and dated clear glass jar. Use them for any number of Pagan purposes, including to bleach white ceremonial magic or Druidic ritual garb, as a substitute for sand or dirt in censers, and to add their power during subsequent spells.

SAMHAIN

Use these ashes to appease restless Spirits by sprinkling them atop gravesites or memorial altars or to signify mourning during a Rite for the Departed Soul.

---

152 https://www.everplans.com/articles/hindu-funeral-traditions.

Toss Samhain ashes to foretell future events by the pattern that they make. Close your eyes and cast them to the ground. Draw random marks in them with a burin, chopstick, or stylus and interpret the meaning of the symbols produced.

Or, toss Samhain Sabbat ashes onto a bigot's yard to encourage them to relocate. Witches' New Year is a goodly time to press for positive change in this fashion.

YULE

Use past Yule Sabbat ashes in future Yule Sabbat rites to ensure that the Sun rises the morn after the longest night of the year—the winter solstice.[153] Spread them as a base for laying the Yule log firewood atop. Before setting the blaze, draw in them the ancient symbol for the Sun—a circle with a dot in its center.

Nourish the baby Sun God by adding Yule fire ashes to the offering of feast food and liquor spirits made to the God/desses during the Cakes & Wine ceremony that follows spellwork.

IMBOLC

Also called "the Festival of Torches", this holy occasion during the depth of winter is when Witches revere the time of new beginnings.

Propitiate the Goddess Bhride[154] to usher in spring soon by making a traditional "Bhride's bed." Make a layer of Sabbat ashes inside a basket or on a platter. Add soft grasses atop the base of ashes. Use cornhusks[155] to fashion a poppet simulacrum of the Goddess, rest Her on the bed, and place the bed near your home's entrance doorway. Exit the premises and then quickly reenter saying:

"BRIDGET, BRIDGET, COME IN, THY BED IS READY."[156]

Help Bhride dispel winter darkness by burning one or three candles near Her bed.[157]

ALTERNATIVES: You can also use ashes produced in fires at this time for the following:

---

153 Stay awake all night and witness the sunrise to ensure that your spell took hold and will succeed.
154 Pronounce as "breed."
155 Readily available in grocery stores and Hispanic *bodegas*, for many folk use them to wrap tamales.
156 Richard Cavendish, *Man, Myth and Magic: An Illustrated Encyclopedia of the Supernatural*, Vol. 14. BPC Publishing Ltd./Petty and Sons Ltd., Leeds and London, 1970.
157 Traditionally, Witches would burn candles near Bhride's bed throughout the night. However, if you don't want to burn unattended flame, you may elect to substitute safer votive candles in containers, or battery-operated tea lights.

* Aid new ventures, such as when trying to cement a new relationship, enable you to make a goodly impression during a job interview, when first attending college, or to minimize the challenges of relocating.

* Promote plant growth by sprinkling Imbolc ashes in compost to fertilize a newly planted tree line, property boundary, rosebushes, or food seeds in a backyard garden.

OSTARA

Ash from this Sabbat can help you conceive a child by sprinkling some beneath your bed or putting some of it in a paper envelope secreted inside your pillowcase and sleeping atop it. Fold Ostara ashes into food coloring or dyes to add texture and patterns when decorating Easter eggs.[158]

BELTANE

Widely considered some of the most auspicious Sabbat ashes, these are renowned for packing a powerful punch capable of boosting any spell. Indeed, they fairly vibrate with high semi-sexual energy that can enable your spell intent and grant your magical workings a wicked goodly *oomph!*

Mix Beltane ashes with pyrotechnic agents to add color and kick to gathering or Coven rite balefires.

LITHA

Ashes produced when the Sun is at His zenith can heal folk.

Fill a censer with Litha ashes and use it as a base on which to burn solar-type incense such as copal, frankincense, or sunflower seeds, etc. Better yet, provide comfort to and encourage the convalescence and recovery of the ill by making and air-drying a yellow wax poppet that represents them and then laying the simulacrum down atop a bed of these Sabbat ashes.

ALTERNATIVE: You can oppose dangerous cold winter weather conditions by using Litha Sabbat ashes as a ritual spell component say, by tossing some in a Strega Witch fire.

---

158 The Christian word "Easter" is a stark example of "language drift," derived from the original Pagan term "Ostara."

LAMMAS

Toss plant matter into this Sabbat fire to later use the resultant ashes to naturally "veggie dye" magical garb in the colors associated with the first harvest. Examples include the following:

* Powdered goldenseal plant yields yellow.

* Crushed madder plant reveals red.

* Pulverized woad bathes things blue.

* Dried spinach squashed in a mortar makes things green.

* Concentrated wet coffee grounds dyes things brown.

* Chopped black walnut soaked long in water or alcoholic Spirits makes a black color.

* Pokeberry juice creates royal purple.

MABON

Use these ashes as a component in Pagan spells to conjure abundance/prosperity, collected during this second harvest Sabbat of grain that sustains us during the notorious "starving time" of winter.

ALTERNATIVE: Or you can nourish harvested fields by sowing Mabon ashes on the ground to replenish ground nutrients and to protect against winter-weather stripping and sundry.

ASH-BLOWING SPELLS

Movies routinely feature the formulaic plot device of a conjuring man blowing ashes in someone's face to make them a zombie. Although this is literally "in your face" overt (Witches are more cunning than to face a target in this fashion), the act itself is a venerable magical practice.

Blowing out a candle insults the Element Fire for sure, but blowing its ashes doesn't, and can visibly show us an instant response regarding our desires depending on the way they waft in the air.

BLESSED BID[159]

On a Monday or Friday at sunset or midnight, preferably during a waxing or full moon, burn sage or a similarly high-note scented incense such as lotus or eucalyptus. Blow its ashes toward the direction in which you want someone to be happy, healthy, lucky, wealthy, or wise. Face East and burn a white candle and balsam incense, or face West and burn a blue candle and cypress incense.

GONE GUST

Blow ashes away from you to banish a dangerous or hurtful person, problem, or habit, etc. Could be a person, problem, habit, or whatnot.

At midnight on a Saturday, go adoors and face the direction where the person lives, the place the problem is coming from, or the direction of the Element with which the issue corresponds. Hold sacred ashes in your left hand and mentally, visually, resolutely push the issue. Feel the breeze of sweet relief. Follow through by refusing all future contact with that person, or taking physical measures to fix the problem or exercising resolute willpower to break your habit.

---

159 In Witchcraft, the term is pronounced "BLESS-ed Be," not "Blessed" as Christians say.

BIBLIOGRAPHY

Advanced Candle Magick: More Spells and Rituals for Every Purpose. Raymond Buckland, Llewellyn Publishing, 2002.

Candles: Creating Candles Like a Pro. Samantha Nobani, Independent Publishing Platform, 2014.

Candle Lighting Encyclopedia. Tina Kand, Boaz Printing, 1991.

Candlelight Spells: The Modern Witch's Book of Spellcasting, Feasting, and Natural Healing. Gerina Dunwich, Citadel Press, 1993.

Candlemaking The Natural Way: 31 Projects Made with Soy, Palm & Beeswax. Rebecca Ittner, Lark Crafts, Sterling Publishing Co. Inc., 2011.

Encyclopedia of Goddesses and Heroines. Patricia Monaghan, Greenwood, 2009.

Encyclopedia of Gods: Over 2,500 Deities of the World. Michael Jordan, Facts on File, 1993.

Fire Eating: A Manual of Instruction. Benjamin "Garth" Mack and Brandon McKinney, Kindle eBook, 2011.

Fire Magic. Clettis V. Musson, Brownstone Classic, 1952, Wildside Press, 2007.

Folklore and Odysseys of Food and Medicinal Plants: An Illustrated Sourcebook of Therapeutic, Magical, Exotic and Nutritional Uses with 200 Illustrations from Ancient Herbals and Old Manuscripts. Ernst and Johanna Lehner, Farrar, Straus, and Giroux, 1973.

Food in England. Dorothy Hartley, Little, Brown, 2006.

Gods, Demigods and Demons: An Encyclopedia of Greek Mythology. Bernard Evslin, Scholastic Inc., 1975.

Helping Yourself with White Witchcraft. Al G. Manning, Parker Publishing Co., Inc., 1972.

Kitchen Witch's Guide to Brews and Potions. Patricia Telesco (Marian Singer), Career Press/Kindle, 2008. *Lost Country Life.* Dorothy Hartley, Pantheon Books, 1979.

Man, Myth & Magic: An Illustrated Encyclopedia of the Supernatural Published Every Wednesday, Vol. 14, BPC Publishing Ltd./Petty and Sons Ltd., Leeds and London, 1970.

Papri Graecae Magicae in Translation Including the Demotic Spells. Greek Magical Papyri. Hans Dieter Betz, 1996.

The Book of Practical Candle Magic. Leo Vinci, Red Wheel/Weiser/Conari, 2015.

The Complete Book of Incense, Oils, and Brews. Scott Cunningham, Llewellyn Publications, 1991, 2001.

The Complete Candlemaker: Techniques, Projects, Inspirations. Norma Coney, Lark Books, 1997.

The Goodly Spellbook. Olde Spells for Modern Problems. Lady Passion (Dixie Deerman) and *Diuvei (Steven Rasmussen), Sterling Publishing, 2005, 2014.

The Handmade Candle. Alison Jenkins, Story Books, 2001.

The Magic of Fire: Hearth Cooking: One Hundred Recipes for the Fireplace or Campfire. William Rubel (author and publisher), 2004.

The Magic in Food: Legends, Lore, and Spellwork. Scott Cunningham, Llewellyn's Practical Magick, 1990.

Pow-Wows; Or, Long Lost Friend: A Collection Of Mysterious And Invaluable Arts And Remedies, For Man As Well As Animals, With Many Proofs of their value and efficacy in healing diseases, ect, [sic] *the greater part of which was never published until they appeared in print for the first time in the U.S. in the year 1820.* Johanm Georg Hohman. English translation 1828.

The Rituals of Dinner. The Origins, Evolution, Eccentricities, and Meaning of Table Manners. Margaret Visser, Harper Perennial, 1992.

Simply Savory: Magical and Medieval Recipes. Lady Passion (Dixie Deerman), oldenworks. org/smashwords.com, 2010.

Wicca Candle Magic. Witchcraft for the Solitary Practitioner. Ginger Valentine, CreateSpace Independent Publishing/Kindle, 2015.

OTHER BOOKS BY THE AUTHOR

Ask-A-Priestess: Magic Answers and Spells From a Real Witch (Lady Passion, Smashwords. com, 2009).

The Goodly Spellbook: Olde Spells for Modern Problems (Lady Passion and *Diuvei, Sterling Publishing Company, 2005, 2014).

Italian translation: *Il Libro Degli Incantesemi: Antique Formule Magiche Per Risolvere Problemi Attuali* (Lady Passion and *Diuvei, Gruppo Editoriale Armenia, Milan, 2006, 2015).

Pagan Prisoner Advocate's Guide (Lady Passion/Dixie Deerman, oldenworks.org, 2013).

Rituals & Sabbats: Sacred Rites & Seasonal Celebrations (Lady Passion and *Diuvei, Sterling Publishing Company, 2017).

Simply Savory: Magical and Medieval Recipes (Lady Passion, smashworks.org, 2010).

INDEX

ABOUT THE AUTHOR

Lady Passion is an experienced blind seer, a registered nurse since 1988, High Priestess of Coven Oldenwilde since 1994, and an internationally bestselling authoress since 2005. Her magical specialties are divination, making magical medicines, and conducting elaborate public rituals.

Lady Passion's successful spiritual, environmental, and social justice activism is documented online, such as her elimination of North Carolina's antidivination law, protection of registered nurses from being fired for advocating for patients' rights (*Deerman v. Beverly California Corp.*), saving of century-old trees on a public park and an old haunted stone jail beneath them, and much more.

The Lady counsels folk worldwide and frequently works magic for the media such as Extra!, CNN, and BBC London. She lives snugly in her three-story Covenstead in the bowl of Asheville surrounded by breathtaking Appalachian Blue Ridge Mountains.

Readers may contact Lady Passion through her Coven's popular Wiccan websites: wiccans.org, oldenwilde.org, and oldenworks.org.